AFRICAN VILLAGE

AFRICAN VILLAGE

LIVING IN A SWAZI HOMESTEAD

MARGO RUSSELL

First published in 2001 by Channel 4 Books, an imprint of Pan Macmillan Ltd,
Pan Macmillan, 20 New Wharf Road, London N1 9RR, Basingstoke and Oxford.

Associated companies throughout the world

www.panmacmillan.com

ISBN 0 7522 1990 1

9 7 5 3 1 2 4 6 8

A CIP catalogue record for this book is available from the British Library.

Designed by seagulls
Photography © Francesca Yorke
Colour reproduction by Speedscan
Printed and bound by New Interlitho, Spa, Milan

RDF MEDIA

This book accompanies the television series *Going Native*
made by RDF Media for Channel 4.
Executive producer: Stephen Lambert
Producer: Helen Richards

Acknowledgement is made to the many people who, wittingly and unwittingly,
contributed to this book; in particular the Nestor family of London and their Swazi
hosts, the Shongwe family of Ekudzeni; Jo Crawley, Stephen Lambert and Helen Richards
of RDF Television; and the rest of the Swaziland film crew: Steve Anderson, Bridget
Bakokodie, Sally Braithwaite, Dirk Nel, Jon Ormrod and Aidan Woodward. The
Swaziland Strategic Communications Consultants, especially Andrew Masina;
also Ernest Dlamini, Lamswati Dlamini, Thobile Dlamini, Sibongile
Magongo, Bheki Maseko, Jenni Russell and Martin Russell.

CONTENTS

PROLOGUE

It seemed Daniel was going to like Africa.

When the pick-up finally stopped on the soft, red-earth road above the Shongwe homestead, and Chloe whined that she wanted to stretch her legs, and Lynn was too hot, and Robert went jogging down the incline – part explorer, part fitness fanatic – while Callum gingerly tested the feel of the road under his bare feet, then hopped back into the minibus to inspect the soles for damage, Daniel sat very quietly looking out over the still, green valley.

Above them the Mdzimba mountains reached into the blue sunset sky, boulder upon boulder. Below them the roofs of the homestead buildings made a pattern against the swept red-earth yard, circles of grass and rectangles of corrugated iron, etched with the long, black shadows of the day's end. In the centre, like a fortress, the uneven poles of the cattle kraal, mighty branches from felled trees, stood grey and stern against the damp, dark, dung floor. Bright-green maize plants stood summer-high on the small undulating fields that ran down to the river. Beyond, on the other side of the valley, tiny mud-walled houses glowed under their rusting tin roofs. Two small trees cast long shadows across the yard. The Nestors could not see the Shongwes, waiting in excitement to receive them in the shadow of the Great Hut.

'I wish I could stay here,' said Daniel, pensively.

'You are going to stay here,' said the driver. 'That's what this is all about.'

'I mean for ever,' said Daniel.

INTRODUCTION

The idea of asking a British family to live for three months as part of a rural African homestead had been mooted by a television production company about six months earlier. Africa was having a bad press: famines in Ethiopia and northern Kenya; wars, refugees and starvation in Sudan and the Horn; insurgents in Guinea and Sierra Leone; floods and homelessness in Mozambique; riots and killings in Zimbabwe; AIDS cutting a swathe through the population from one end of the continent to the other. Was there any good news?

The good news was surely in the uneventful day-to-day ability of most ordinary rural people to get on with their lives, heedless of the headlines; to cultivate their fields with hoes or ploughs and plant their carefully saved seed; to make rain with their medicine men at times of drought; to ensure the judicious distribution of the family food and nurture of the children; to make love and take care of the consequences; to raise the next generation cheerfully and equip them with these survival skills. If a British family were to go and share this experience, and then share their own experience with the television cameras, that would be news – good news – about Africa.

A suitable country had to be found, preferably one that was remote from war and insurrection, where political stability meant that food was adequate, where disease was not so rife as to be threatening, where people were as content with their lot as people ever are. It needed to be a country not so drawn into the international market that its distinctively African way of doing things had been eroded, but not so remote from that market that filming would be difficult. There were several possible places. In the end Swaziland was selected: a small independent kingdom, about four-fifths of the size of Wales, with a population of one million, tucked between the eastern side of South Africa and Mozambique.

৪০ ৫৪

If you fly into Swaziland from Johannesburg, you look down on to rolling hills covered in gum and pine plantations, divided by winding earth roads and lazy brown rivers, studded with rocky outcrops where, amid scattered boulders, indigenous plants still survive the greedy grasp of the paper makers. Then suddenly the contoured Swazi fields appear, row upon row of narrow, winding strips, marking the fall of the hills like a topographer's map, green with maize in summer, edged with blond grass in winter. Tiny roofs of rusted tin and dull grey thatch cluster near trees on cleared patches of earth. Red roads snake their way between and over hills. Low mountains rise abruptly towards you as the plane descends, skimming a river full of rocks, a field of grey pineapples. The plane roars and shudders to a halt beside the low airport building in its small, carefully tended garden. Strelitzia, pawpaws and plumbago are in flower. The air is warm and damp and filled with the smell of hot tarmac and aeroplane fuel. This is Matsapha, the industrial heart of Swaziland.

By Swazi standards, this part of the country is densely settled. The road from the airport is lined with billboards advertising furniture, takeaway food, cement, beer and the newest South African chainstore. Makeshift stalls sell undersized fruit in plastic bags. Handpainted signs offer the services of welders, mechanics and hairdressers. Tall grass and flowering weeds hide the litter along the unkempt verges, busy with schoolchildren and wandering goats and cattle. The road bustles with ramshackle buses, lorries spewing black fumes, fast cars and crammed minibuses. This is a country where most people walk, skirting puddles after rain, dodging erratic drivers who veer off the tarmac, impatiently overtaking on the wrong side.

The airport and the industrial area lie on Swaziland's central plateau, its midlands. To the west the land rises sharply. What appears to be a mountain range is actually the edge of an escarpment. The high western side of the country is cool, with poor soil and lots of rain. In summer, low clouds hang on the hills for days, the thick mist obscuring everything. Invasive wattle trees, encouraged by the British, break the monotony of grassland. Historically Swazis have tended to steer clear of this high land. Its scant population has been thinned still further by the huge timber plantations, established in the late 1940s, which now take up great swathes of Swazilands's high country.

The low-lying east of the country, by contrast, is fertile, dry and flat, covered in thorn bushes. The rainfall is uncertain making growing your own food precarious. Cotton plantations, cattle ranches, game reserves and sugar plantations flourish, all the preserve of those with capital to invest. Incongruously ugly mines working a low-grade coal seam offer valued employment to the local population.

Swazis sensibly concentrate themselves in the area that lies between these two contrasting regions. In the midlands the climate is warm, the rains fairly dependable and the soil good. It is undulating, hilly country, strewn with boulders, cut by rivers fed from hundreds of perennial mountain streams and springs, some of them hot. The soil is often red, while the vegetation is subtropical and lush in sheltered valleys and ravines. The rains come in summer in fierce electrical storms, occasionally killing livestock and people. The winters are warm, sunny and dry. Here the succession of Swazi kings ruled from a series of capitals, as each new king is required to establish his own. The nineteenth-century white settlers, the Afrikaners, also established their capital of corrugated iron shops in these temperate midlands. They called it Bremersdorp; it is now called Manzini after a famous Swazi prince. The British, who took political control of the country as a protectorate at the start of the twentieth century, established their capital in the cool highlands. Mbabane is still the administrative capital. As befits a modern capital, it rises higher each year, as new multi-storeyed buildings are put up by the government for its sprawling bureaucracy, and by investors hopeful of attracting the legions of non-governmental organizations, foreign trade missions, embassies and international firms that gather in all African capitals.

Just a four-hour drive by car from Johannesburg, Swaziland is never short of creature comforts. At the same time, it is a thoroughly African country – one of the few African kingdoms to have withstood the tide of independence. Swazi enthusiasm for kingship is in large measure the consequence of King Sobhuza's struggle against colonialism. Five years after the country's independence in 1968, to the general rejoicing of 90 per cent of the population, Sobhuza rejected the Westminster-style constitution that the British had foisted on them and seized absolute power of a traditional African king. People loved and revered him; when he drove along the road in his ageing Studebaker, those at the roadside dropped to their knees and bowed their heads until he passed. When he died in 1982, after a sixty-one-year reign, the whole country went into mourning. Men and virgins shaved their heads and nobody ploughed their land for three months. In 1986 the present king, Mswati the Third, was installed as the Lion, *Ngwenyama*, in a colourful ceremony attended by several heads of state. His mother became the queen, *Ndlovukati*, or the Elephant. For days the country feasted in celebration. Oxen from the royal herd were generously slaughtered and, to the amazement of visiting diplomats, roasted whole.

Europeans, Americans and white South Africans form less than 1 per cent of the population They live in Western enclaves, in the one-third of the country where land is bought and sold, where familiar rules of commerce prevail, where capital is invested and profits are made, where labour is cheap and workers queue outside factory gates whenever there is a rumour of expanding production. Residence and work permits for outsiders are grudgingly given and easily withdrawn. They are not allowed to buy property without special dispensation.

A colonial law of 1916 prohibits all outsiders from living in the other two-thirds of the country. This is the king's land, *inda-woyenkhosi*. Government papers refer to it as Swazi Nation Land. This land is held by the king on behalf of the people and administered by some 160 hereditary chiefs. Land allocation is the basis of the chiefs' power. With their councils, they are responsible for the equitable distribution of homestead sites to married Swazi men and for controlling who lives in their chiefdoms. Here, on the king's land, people establish their rural homesteads, clusters of small houses or huts for the extended family's accommodation, and sufficient adjoining land to grow the family's basic food, maize. Those families rich enough to own cattle – about half of all rural homesteads – also build a *kraal* close to their houses.

Nation Land is the central institution of Swazi society. It is the great equalizer. In principle, every Swazi (rich or poor) has access to it, directly or indirectly. Nobody pays for it; no rates are paid on it. The only obligation is tribute labour, *kuhlehla*, when summoned on behalf of the chief or king. This land is highly valued, not so much for the food it produces (though this is considerable: half the people in Swaziland grow all of their maize on it most of the time) as for the place it gives people to live on, to retreat to, to belong to. It gives them a community. Here they can build the house of their choice, from mud-walled, thatched hut to elegant mansion. This is a new freedom. For almost half a century domestic building on the king's land was 'on hold', pending the rational resettlement of people, to make the best use of the soils. This resettlement has now been completed. The last decade has seen a tremendous boom in the number of permanent block-built houses. They are less charming to the outsider than traditional buildings, but are enjoyed by their inhabitants as a symbol of their achievement. A traditional house can be built with nothing but wood, mud and grass; a block-house costs money. It is a status symbol. It is also more durable, less liable to infestation by insects and rodents, and less likely to go up in smoke.

Socially the homestead consists of a great many related people, not all of whom choose to live there all of the time. Here, daily life is regulated by unwritten customary law. The oldest married man is usually the homestead head, though when he dies his widow is likely to act as head until her son is considered man enough to succeed him. The old are always more important than the young, who are very numerous, the Swazi birth rate being among the highest in the world.

Everything that happens in the homestead must be reported to the head, whose opinion and permission must be sought on all important matters. Sick children sometimes die because their mothers are afraid to take them to hospital without his permission. His name is never spoken aloud. His daughters-in-law must maintain a respectful distance from him at all times. Although they bring him food, they are not allowed to see him eat. It is he who decides how the fields should be allocated within the family. He disposes of any agricultural surplus and chooses how to spend the proceeds. He expects his sons to support him from their earnings, and mostly they do so. One of the charming conditions for income-tax rebates in Swaziland is having an aged living parent, support of whom is taken for granted in Swaziland, just as support of infant children is taken for granted in Britain.

It was on the king's land that the British family would have to live, if they were to experience fully contemporary African rural life.

CHAPTER ONE
accepting the challenge

Robert Nestor, a London lorry driver, saw the flyer one night in September 2000 at Streatham public swimming baths. He was taking his usual evening swim after a workout at the gym: 'Channel 4 are looking for a family to take to Africa, to live in an African village for three months. Are you up to the challenge? Phone this number.'

He brought the flyer home to his wife Lynn, announcing, 'You say you never go anywhere – this will stop you moaning!' A busy mother of three and a nurse at a local general medical practice in West Norwood, where they live, Lynn found the idea instantly appealing and rang in. 'It was an answerphone. I don't remember saying anything dramatic that would make her answer my call. It was really basic: "Hello. I'm replying to the advert. Our family would be very interested in going to Africa. Our family consists of Lynn, thirty-seven; Robert, thirty-six; Daniel, twelve; Chloe, eight; and Callum, four; and we really would like to go, so give us a ring back." And somebody phoned back about an hour later.' The Nestors were one of 300 families to answer the advert, and, following interviews with Robert, Lynn and the children, they were finally told that they had been chosen six weeks after making the call.

Robert had always wanted to go to Africa. He grew up in Hackney, in London's East End, the son of Caribbean immigrants

(opposite)
The Nestor family
in London. From top
to bottom, Robert, Lynn,
Daniel, Chloe and Callum.

Father and son, London.

from Dominica, who settled in London in the 1950s. His mother was a nurse, his father a carpenter. His parents split up when he was six. He stayed with his mother, but remained close to his father and his three younger half-brothers. After leaving school at sixteen he drifted from job to job before meeting Lynn when he was twenty-two. His mother was happy that he had met someone to settle down with, and Lynn was soon pregnant with Daniel. In 1991, when Daniel was four, and after much procrastination on both sides, they got married in a church in Folkestone. There was no money for a honeymoon, but someone lent them a caravan at Hastings for four nights and they went on a day-trip to Belgium while Lynn's mother babysat.

In 1999 Robert got his present job driving for a builders' merchant in Fulham in west London. He gets up shortly after six o'clock each day and is the first one in the family to leave for work, but his day really starts when his work ends and he reaches the gym. 'I go to the gym three, sometimes four, days a week. It's close to where I work. I train a lot of amateur boxers and then I do a little bit of training myself. After that I probably go swimming in Streatham.'

Life with a washing machine; Lynn at home.

He doesn't get home until ten and buys himself takeaway food on the way home. The gym burns up his excessive energy – he sometimes runs to work – and soaks up his anger. 'A lot of people walk around angry. They don't know why they're angry. You have to channel that aggression and strength in some direction.' It also answers his passion to keep fit. 'I look at other people the same age as me and I think, "How can you let yourself go like that!" I want to be an active pensioner. That's what I'm working towards.' The gym is also his retreat, 'somewhere to go when things ain't going right. You just want to get away from everything. This is the only place I can come and say, "Yeah, this is my place." I go there and work it off. I come out and feel all right. Some people go to church. The gym is my fortress and my solitude.'

The Nestors live in the house in which Lynn grew up, a modest three-up, two-down end-of-terrace house built about 150 years ago. They bought it from her mother when her father died. It had belonged to her grandmother before that. It's on a busy main road, but they like its convenience. 'It's opposite a park, there's a pub six houses away, there's a shop all of ten seconds' walk from our front door.' It's a cheerful, congested place, with brightly painted walls and staircase and shelves over-flowing with possessions. Chloe and Callum share a room. Daniel has a tiny room to himself, which he's going to have to give to Chloe soon; she's getting old enough to need a girl's room to herself.

Lynn prides herself on their active social life in London. She sees herself as the hospitable hub of a small, close-knit commu-nity of active Christians in West Norwood. She holds a weekly Bible study group in her house on Wednesdays, her free day. Their children go to church schools: Chloe and Callum to a Church of England primary school that Lynn herself attended as a child. 'It's literally a one-minute walk away.' Daniel goes to a Catholic secondary school, from which he is fetched by car on most days. As a nurse in a local practice situated five minutes from home, Lynn meets a lot of people she already knows from church and school. 'Everybody knows everybody.' Many of the people she sees on the streets are those she grew up with. Daniel's best friend is the son of an old classmate of hers. 'People do move away from West Norwood, but they tend to come back again. I moved away for five years when I went nursing. I had to. But as soon as I could I came back south.'

Lynn describes her house as 'an absolute madhouse. At any one time there are at least three of somebody else's children there. My friends come and go all day long. They just come in and put the kettle on. Make them-selves at home, basically. If you come to my house you look after yourself. That seems to work very well.' She likes to be busy. She works four days a week and in the evenings is often out at meetings in school and church. She spends her spare time shopping and socializing. 'I nip down the road in the car and do some shopping. I pop over to a friend.

I'm not tied to the house.' She makes herself useful helping people. Robert mocks her for this. He calls her 'a soft touch'.

Robert could not wait to get to Africa. Ever since he could remember he had heard people talking about it. 'That's where every black person on the planet has come from originally.' He thought Africa had had a hard time. 'Other parts of the world haven't been used and abused the way Africa's been used.' He was boundlessly optimistic about going to stay there for ten weeks. 'I know it's not as backward as people have tried to tell me it is.' He thought the people would be very friendly and welcoming and hoped to make some good friends. 'I don't think there's going to be anything I don't like about the place.'

Lynn thought differently. 'Robert's going to find it the biggest shock. If anybody's going to want to come home, it's going to be Robert.'

He thought she misjudged him. 'Lynn only sees me as her husband. She doesn't see what I'm like outside the home, communicat-ing with all sorts of people. She doesn't see me at work. I see going to Africa as work. It's not a holiday. I don't expect it to be a holiday.'

Lynn had been to Africa before on a pack-age holiday to Gambia. She felt that she knew what to expect. She was looking forward to quiet evenings under the stars and planned to do a lot of reading. She was tired of being a superwoman, juggling her job and the domes-tic chores, 'running around in circles, tearing yourself apart'. She was looking forward to being a full-time housewife and mother. 'There are clearly defined roles over there. Everybody knows what they have to do. The women are quite content in their role. It's something I look forward to. A rest, really.'

Daniel and Chloe were consulted by their parents about the project. Thirteen-year-old

Daniel before relinquishing his computer.

Daniel – a big, quiet, thoughtful boy – was unreservedly enthusiastic from the start. He would get to understand the African side of himself. 'I know where the white side of my family comes from because I live with it every day. I don't know where my black side comes from. I'd be in Africa if it wasn't for the slave trade. I've read about it and seen it on telly, but,' he laughed, 'the closest I've ever come to it is Hackney!' All he would miss was his bed. He thought he'd get used to their food within a week – 'rice and yams,' he said confidently, but mistakenly. His one anxiety was language. 'I won't know what they're talking about.' As for luggage, he would take a games compendium and a football. 'Keep it nice and light.'

Eight-year-old Chloe, her imagination informed by famines and refugees seen on television, wondered, dramatically, whether she should wear rags like African children. She thought of taking them her broken toys: she'd seen that idea on a television programme. 'We've got all this stuff and they've got nothing. They've got no TV. They haven't even got ironing boards.' She wanted to try going to school out there, but wondered if they'd have any pencils and paper. She had a long list of things she was going to miss: her bedroom, her toilet, her toys, her swimming lessons, her rabbit, her guinea pig, her friends. She thought the children in Africa might not want to make friends with her. She expected to dislike the food and thought she might starve, but

would probably eat the food if she was 'really really hungry'. She would take two soft toys with her, one to remind her of her best friend and one to remind her of home. She was planning to hug them if she got upset.

Four-year-old Callum said, 'Can I feed the lions? Will I be able to feed the lions? I want to feed the lions,' until his family threatened, 'We'll feed *you* to the lions', which quite upset him.

Afterwards Lynn said, 'We had a family consultation, but the children didn't really have any part in the decision. It was our decision; they had to go along with it.'

The Nestors were delighted to have been selected. 'We were really keen to do it, and most of our friends – most of our good friends – were genuinely pleased.' Others were more sceptical. 'People I don't know so well just think we're completely mad. We must be off our heads.' Some, like Lynn's employer, thought they must be being paid huge sums. 'He cannot

understand that I'm doing this for the experience. He really cannot get to grips with it at all.'

Robert describes such sceptics as people with 'a stereotypical view of Africa. They watch too much *Tarzan*. They don't look further than their front doors. Where they live in London, that's as far as they want to go.'

Lynn dismissed such people as 'caught up in practical things, like toilet facilities, no electricity, no – you know – running water', which she described as 'all minor details. They're thinking, "No, I can't do that."'

The Nestor family, by contrast, set out as 'can dos'.

(opposite)
Chloe in the room she shares with Callum, surrounded by some of the things she thought she would miss in Africa.

(below)
Callum with one of his paintings.

CHAPTER TWO
finding a swazi community

Strangers are not readily welcomed into any Swazi home. The unfamiliar is always dangerous. Outsiders very rarely enter a Swazi house, which matters less than it might, since entertaining is always an outdoor affair – grass mats are unrolled in the shade of a tree or a building. Hospitality is minimal, reserved for special occasions. Houses are private places.

As with the homestead, so with the community. The laws of Swaziland prohibit the overnight stay of non-Swazis on the king's land without the express approval of the chief or king. It therefore came as a surprise that a team of Swazi consultants were able, at very short notice, to compile a shortlist of six homesteads, all willing to offer temporary membership to a British family whom they had never seen, and all anticipating no major objection from community or chief. 'We start where we are known,' the consultants explained. 'We all have our rural roots; we all have our chiefs. We each go to our own areas where we know the people and are known by them. We explain the advantage to the homestead of receiving the strangers; that they will be well paid for their hospitality. The chief is happy to see the homestead profiting from the situation. He will not object.'

The unexpected difficulty was a logistical one. The British family had to have an authentic rural African experience of what has come, rather thoughtlessly, to be known as underdevelopment.

(opposite)
The Shongwe homestead at Ekudzeni. Bright green maize plants stand summer-high on the small undulating fields that run down to the river.

The crew, however, was to have none of this; they needed, as a minimum, electricity to charge the batteries for their equipment on location, and to be able to work at night, reviewing the day's filming, checking the day's sound and transferring rushes to tape. They also needed a space, to live and work in, such as is rarely found in a Swazi rural area, and even then is not for hire, since the king's land is granted to people only for their own use. Commercial enterprises on such land are strictly controlled through the chiefs. Nobody builds on the king's land with the intention of renting, except around the edges of the quickly growing towns, where new economic pressures are eroding older rules and practices. In short, there is simply no rentable housing in the rural areas, and if there were, it would be illegal to let it to non-Swazis.

The crew was going to be forced to live in one of the three bigger towns, where appropriate housing could be found. At the same time they needed to be close enough to the British family to make daily filming practicable with no more than three hours each day travelling. Given the rough state of minor rural roads and the fact that shooting was going to coincide with the rainy season, a suitable homestead had to be found within forty miles of a town. The search for a location had to begin again, still working through personal contacts of the consultants, but this time within a much more limited geographical range.

The closer a rural area is to a town, the more densely settled it will become. Swazis have long been drawn into the fringes of the global economy. It is in the towns that wage work can be found, as well as markets for the items that people can produce at home: from baskets and bananas to ceremonial wigs and porridge spoons. People are quick to see the advantage of having their rural base within easy reach of one of the towns.

The Mdzimba mountains.

All those with some hereditary claim to land in such an area are likely to remain there, exploiting its opportunities of access. The people in such areas are likely to be better off than more remote rural dwellers. Houses will be more substantial, and more of them will be built of durable materials like concrete blocks and metal windows, rather than branches, stones, mud and grass. They are more likely to have electricity because the power lines will be closer, and the cost of the connection accordingly less. They are more likely to be served by a reasonable public transport system, because more of the journey into town will be on tarmac roads, cutting down on bus owners' costs and pushing up their profits.

The production company looked for a homestead that lay just beyond this band of privilege. They were not wanting to bring a British family 6,000 miles to live in some relatively privileged African commuter belt. Eventually they found a homestead belonging to the Shongwe family at Ekudzeni, some twenty-five miles from Swaziland's fastest-growing town, Manzini.

The Shongwes have always lived at the foot of the Mdzimba mountains at Ekudzeni, 'the far-away place'. Their land lies some six miles beyond Zombodze, the old royal capital, where Queen Labotsibeni ruled the Swazis for thirty-two years until the installation of her grandson, King Sobhuza the Second. His embalmed body crouches in solemn state in a secret cave up in the mountains, with other past kings and princes, their parched skins and whitened bones wrapped in softest sheepskin. Their spirits hover over the Mdzimba mountains. Uniformed soldiers camp at Zombodze to stop inquisitive strangers from trying to find these tombs. But

Swazis know better than to annoy the powerful spirits of the dead.

The first government school in Swaziland was built at Zombodze in 1908, so that young Swazi aristocrats could become literate without being subjected to tireless missionary pressures for conversion to Christianity. The road to Zombodze is an old one, and much travelled. Fewer people have cause to take the road through Zombodze to Ngamanzi, fewer still go beyond it to Ekudzeni. There are no buses into Ekudzeni. When the Shongwes, like many people of Ekudzeni, want to go anywhere, they always start by walking. Their children often walk six miles each way to school. People coming and going to work or to the shops have to walk at least two miles to catch the nearest bus.

In the early mornings, when the day is cool, it is a lovely walk. The red-earth road rises and falls along the spurs of the mountain. From the breast of each foothill you look down on to the wide green valley. In each dip clear water tumbles down from the mountain. On sticky afternoons the children trudging home from school stop and strip, and splash in the streams. Small boys bring goats to drink, noisily throwing stones and shouting to keep them in line, before herding them back up the steep paths. Girls walk from the streams with plastic buckets of water or wet washing balanced on their heads. Idle oxen and cows stand in the road, stiff-legged, chewing the cud. Once you reach the bus route, the road is wider and busier. People wait, sometimes for hours, for the bus. Women sell fruit, chewing gum and biscuits from makeshift stalls under trees. Expansive customers at the local tavern, or *shebeen*, sit in the shade of a jacaranda tree on boxes and upturned buckets and noisily hail passers-by. This is the centre of the chiefdom.

From left to right, the bachelors' quarters (lilawu), *Robert and Lynn's round house,* gogo *laBhembe's house,* gogo *laBhembe's kitchen, Amos and Thandi's house, Thandi's kitchen and the Great Hut* (indlunkhulu) *with reed screen.*

(opposite)
Umkhulu *Mangedlane Shongwe, head of the homestead and proud father of nineteen children, at his cattle* kraal.

Here, just out of sight, down a track past a church and a pre-school, is the chief's place, *umphakatsi,* where the community regularly meets to discuss matters of local concern.

The Shongwe homestead lies just below the road, where the mountain slope is so steep that you cannot see the few neighbouring houses above it, and the land so undulating that you cannot see the houses beside it. On a square of red, swept earth there are sixteen small buildings, all but one facing east, towards the large cattle *kraal.* They are surrounded by a few livestock pens and, on three sides, by irregular fields that stretch in a patchwork down and across the bordering river and stream. Four of the sixteen buildings are kitchens, suggesting that there are four importantly independent and mature women living in this homestead. One is the Great Hut, the *indlunkhulu.* With its distinctively domed grass roof and its reed screen, it occupies a central position opposite the cattle *kraal.* Here all matters of importance are discussed, in the presence of the ancestors to whom the hut is dedicated. One of the other buildings is a shed and another the bachelor quarters where young unmarried men sleep. Eight of the remaining nine buildings are one-, two- or three-roomed houses, each belonging to one of the mature men of the homestead. The ninth, recently built for a now-deceased grandmother, was available for the British family to stay in.

A homestead is a bit like a club; it has members. Membership is by birth and cannot be withdrawn, but not all members are necessarily there, exercising their membership rights. Absentees may return to the homestead at any time. Like club members, they usually pay their dues. Some homesteads become so big that they split on to separate sites without losing their social cohesion. This has happened to the Shongwe homestead. Two nearby, apparently independent homesteads, physically separate from the main homestead, nevertheless consider themselves part of it. When the family meets in the Great Hut they are expected to be there, in their proper ranked places, a visible part of the homestead hierarchy.

ॐ ಛ

The present head of the homestead, *umkhulu* or grandfather, was born Mangedlane Shongwe at Ekudzeni about sixty-five years ago. His father had two wives. It was a big family, but by his mother there was only one brother, Mcasane, to whom Mangedlane was devoted. They shared the homestead at Ekudzeni all their lives and both took several wives. When Mcasane became homestead head, he invited Mangedlane to stay on. 'The relationship between my brother and myself was so healthy that he did not want me to build my own homestead, but wanted me to stay with him, at home. We stayed together until he died.' This was unusual. More commonly brothers, especially polygamous brothers, will approach the chief and request space to establish their own separate homesteads. Mangedlane became homestead head in 1986 when Mcasane's widow died.

Umkhulu is grey-haired, bright-eyed and strong-limbed. He can still walk the twenty-or-so-mile shortcut from Ekudzeni up the mountain to Mbabane, and he does. He works in Mbabane as a groundsman in one of the government ministries, keeping the rampant indigenous grass in the semblance of a lawn. He never went to school, but he has learnt to write his initials, M. S., which he does slowly, carefully, triumphantly. Eight years ago he was elected to the inner council, the *libandla lencane*, which controls the day-to-day affairs of the Ekudzeni chiefdom. He is a good old-fashioned farmer. Not for him the chemical fertilizers and hybrid seeds so beloved of the agricultural experts that advise the government. He sticks to tried and tested ways, and

Like most Swazi women, this wife of umkhulu *continues to be known by her maiden name. She is* gogo *or grandmother* laKhanyile.

has more than forty cattle. His oldest child is thirty-five; his youngest is still a toddler. Swazis admire fertility, fecundity and sexual agility. *Umkhulu* walks tall.

Of the four wives he has married, only one now lives permanently on the main homestead. This is Elizabeth Khanyile, known as *gogo*, grandmother, laKhanyile. Like most married Swazi women, she continues to be called by her maiden name. When *umkhulu* is away, *gogo* laKhanyile acts as head of the homestead in his place. She is a plump, gentle, dignified woman who began to marry *umkhulu* by getting pregnant in 1969, the year she completed primary school. (Marriage amongst Swazis is a slow process, accomplished in stages over many years.) Of her eight children, only two are still at school. Her three sons are all grown up and working: one of them, Sipho, in South Africa, and the other two, Simon and Mavela, in labouring jobs in Swaziland. They visit the homestead when they can. Two have married and have brought their wives to the homestead; all of them have built houses close to hers. Her house and kitchen form one of the two main focuses of social life in the homestead. Children gather at her doorstep. She now has two daughters-in-law, *makoti*, cooking for her. Her kitchen is a busy place, top-heavy with domestic labour, for *gogo* laKhanyile has five competent unmarried daughters. Mfundvo and Lungile are still in school. Ngabisa has just started work. Patricia has just finished school and has applied to join the police force. Buyisile, the eldest, is the mother of baby Teme. He is *gogo* laKhanyile's first grandchild and is much indulged, for he lives with no fewer than four 'little mothers', *make lomncane*. This is how he will regard and address his mother's younger sisters when he learns to talk.

Another of *umkhulu*'s wives lives close by on a separate site on the other side of the river. This is *gogo* laNkhosi, who was chosen by the people of the Ekudzeni chiefdom to be trained as their rural health motivator, the most junior post in the Ministry of Health – a sort of barefoot health-welfare officer. She is a thin, leathery-looking woman who speaks excellent English shyly. She has four living children, but an extraordinary reproductive history: twins followed by quadruplets, followed by twins. In each case half survived. Only one of her children, Melusi, is still in school, but she has a young household because her two daughters have both had children: one is in the process of getting married. *Gogo* laNkhosi lives with Melusi, her unemployed son Sandile, her daughter Khetsiwe and three of her four grandchildren.

Gogo laBhembe, *umkhulu*'s third wife, whom he began to marry in the 1970s, moved away from the homestead at Ekudzeni in 1993, leaving her house, kitchen and fields behind her. She went to live and work in Mbabane, where *umkhulu* also works. Here she stays, not with him, but with her mother's family, where she used to live as a girl. She still

comes to Ekudzeni with all her children at ploughing, weeding and harvesting times, to tend her fields. There is talk of her permanent return to the homestead later in the year. Her youngest daughter, Phetsile, now three, is *umkhulu*'s youngest child. Her firstborn, Khanyisile, is the first of *umkhulu*'s daughters to have married and moved away; *umkhulu* received six cattle for her. Her three oldest sons, Siboniso, Mark and Njabulo, who grew up at Ekudzeni, still spend a lot of their time there. They sleep in the bachelor quarters, *lilawu*, with Mfana Shongwe, the homestead's herdsman, a very distant relative.

Umkhulu's first wife deserted him years ago, leaving behind Amos, his firstborn child, now a married man of thirty-five. He is based on the homestead but is away at work most of the time. His wife, Thandi laMabuza, makes up for his absence by being cheerfully present on the homestead all the time. She is a prodigious worker. Amos has two children from a former partner. They too are members of the Shongwe homestead, though they live with their mother elsewhere. The Shongwes have been responsible for their schooling and expect Amos's son to build his house at Ekudzeni, and his daughter to bring her marriage cattle to them when she marries.

The most senior man in the homestead, after *umkhulu* himself, is Themba, firstborn son of *umkhulu*'s deceased brother. Themba (now *babe* or father) Shongwe was born in 1960. He came with his mother to live at Ekudzeni when he was twelve years old, having been brought up by his mother's mother, fifty miles away. This is a common Swazi practice. It is the natural consequence of premarital births. Young girls' mothers usually accept and welcome such children until their fathers' kin decide what to do about them. In exactly this spirit *gogo* laKhanyile has welcomed Buyisile's baby, Teme.

Like many other Shongwe children, Themba went to school in Zombodze, walking the twelve-mile round trip each day for five years, until he was 'forced to drop out because of shortage of funds'. Five years later, in 1982, with a driving licence and a pregnant girlfriend, he got his first job as a driver. The girlfriend was Thembi, now his wife and the mother of his eight children. *Babe* Themba Shongwe is now a member of the police force, driving the cars that escort the prime minister wherever he goes. It's a glamorous, demanding job, working for the powerful, with a revolver strapped to his chest, sailing through No Entry signs, sirens sounding, headlights glaring and pennants fluttering in the slipstream. The Nestors never saw this side of him. Themba took leave for six of their ten weeks on the homestead, 'to see how things go'. They only ever saw him in his old casual clothes, digging his vegetable garden, weeding the maize, milking the cows and cracking his whip at recalcitrant oxen yoked to the plough.

His wife, Thembi, is (for the sake of clarity and simplicity) known as *make*, mother, Shongwe: for there are two other wives in the homestead who share her maiden name. She is a buxom woman of thirty-six, with her three younger children always about her, the youngest still latched to her ample breasts. She has only recently given up her responsible position in a women's handicraft business and come to live permanently on the homestead. She speaks English confidently and has been abroad. A few years ago she visited Germany for two weeks as part of a team promoting the export of Swazi handicrafts. Only six of her children live with her. The two eldest, Photisile

and Senzo, have always lived with her mother, in whose homestead they were born before she was taken into the Shongwe homestead as Themba's wife. She says simply, 'I decided to leave them with my mother to help her.' They come to Ekudzeni at weekends and during school vacations. Five of her six younger children are girls. Two are adolescents: Cebsile, slender, pale and retiring, is followed by Xolile, darker and sturdier, with a wicked sense of humour. Welile and Tandzile (also known as Mphondi) are not yet old enough for school. Thandeka is still suckling. When her only other son was born in 1992, they called him Mphendulo, meaning 'answer'. They had been praying for another son.

The second son of *umkhulu*'s brother is Dokta, a father of four, recently returned from the mines in South Africa where he has worked for the past nine years. He is married to pretty, quiet, enigmatic laSibandze. He has built his house and established his fields on a separate site from his brothers. He lives beyond the stream, a few hundred yards from the main homestead. This hiving-off of one brother from another is common. Dokta explains, 'My brothers and I had a lot of children. They used to quarrel with each other. I was tired of staying there.' Two of his children are at primary school; the other two are toddlers, one still small enough to be tied to his mother's back. In 2001 Dokta, dark-skinned and hoarse-voiced, was desperately looking for work. He dreamt of finding a

(opposite)
Babe Themba Shongwe with his wife, Thembi and their youngest daughter, Thandeka, on the front wall of their verandah. They undertook to regard Lynn as a daughter-in law during the duration of the Nestors' stay.

Mandla and Themba Shongwe with their sister's son. The relationship between a child and his mother's brother, umalume, *is particularly close although they are of different clans.*

'sponsor' who would help him to install an irrigation system to lead water from the mountain stream to his fields, so that he could grow sufficient crops to be free of the burden of paid employment for ever. While the Nestors were there his wife left him and his children, and returned to her parents' home.

The third son of *umkhulu*'s brother is Mandla, jilted husband and father of three, whose wife recently took a lover while he was working in the mines in Johannesburg. The Shongwes were negotiating the return of his three children, Mbuso, Nhlanhla and Zakele, to the homestead where they had grown up. It was the empty porch of Mandla's house that was set aside as a sleeping space for the Nestor children while they stayed on the homestead.

It is difficult to establish with any precision how many people there are in any homestead, because people come and go. The Shongwe homestead is no exception. From his own four wives, *umkhulu* has nineteen children, all of whom belong on the homestead. From one of the wives of his dead brother he has another eight children on the homestead; the British would call them nephews and nieces, but the Swazi make no such distinction. *Umkhulu*'s sons and unmarried daughters between them have twenty-three children, his grandchildren. Not all of these fifty-odd descendants stay at Ekudzeni all the time. On week nights when the men are away at work and some of the children are away at school, there may be fewer than fifteen people – mostly children – eating and sleeping at the main homestead, and another thirteen living nearby. At weekends the number at the main homestead readily rises to thirty-three as workers and scholars, *umkhulu* among them, return home. Homestead populations rise and fall with the rhythm of public and school holidays, the expansion and contraction of the labour market and marital disharmonies, as well as births, marriages and deaths.

ༀ ༃

Swazi expectations of the British family were high. The Swazi stereotype of Britons was formed during the protectorate years, when the British colonial servants were charged with putting native interests above those of the grasping settlers, who were by and large South Africans, both English-speaking and Afrikaner. By contrast with the settlers, the British administrators were kind and just, and, with the might of Britannia behind them, powerful. They also tended to be recruited from the educated and upper classes: thoughtful people, often intellectuals.

Umkhulu saw in the arrival of the descendants of such people into their midst the hand of God: the Shongwes were blessed for having been singled out to receive such patrons. *Make* Shongwe was confident 'we are going to learn more from them. We now want the new way, the easy way, how you can build up something, how you can earn money.'

Babe Themba Shongwe declared himself 'shocked and also pleased at the same time. I am happy because it's the first time people are coming from England. I am happy for people to see and to experience how Swazi people are living, because in England I don't think they do weeding. Here we are weeding… I like my nation, actually. We are proud to be Swazis. We like the traditional way. We are all under the king and the chiefs. We are very happy about that. We are a free country.'

Mandla had high hopes that through the Nestors he would be able to travel to England. 'I think we are going to live a good life with them and go to England one day. When you have visitors you wish to see their home country. Is it true that there are no stars in the English night sky?'

Before they arrived *umkhulu* said, 'I have thought deeply about this and realized that this is a blessing from God. In fact I did not know that such a thing could happen, but God intended that these people, whom I myself do not know, should become related to me. I am delighted to have such God-given relatives. I think, one day when I am desperately in need of help, they will provide such help, and come to my rescue in any situation that may face me. I believe they can even take care of my funeral. I believe they will feel welcome and at home because God has sent them to our family.'

What if they were to turn out to be unpleasant, incompatible people? 'I have faith through God that even if a person can come as a wolf in a sheep's skin, because God has sent them, they will identify with us and humble themselves, as they find us humble in this home.' He thought staying in an African homestead would be a transforming process for them.

CHAPTER THREE
an overwhelming reception

(opposite)
The Nestors at home in Robert and Lynn's thatched concrete block house in the Shongwe homestead. In the background is Mandla's house where Daniel, Chloe and Callum slept. Babe Shongwe's empty grain tank lies on its side.

Wise Swazis take the precaution of informing their ancestors of any changes in their affairs: a new job, a new car, a new wife. The ancestors certainly needed to know about the arrival of the Nestors. The Shongwes set about informing their ancestors as soon as possible. Communication with the ancestors is as simple as prayer. The oldest male talks to them, at the cattle *kraal* or in the Great Hut, while at the same time offering them a gift of specially brewed traditional beer, served in a clay pot, and a ritually slaughtered animal, usually a goat.

The brewing was entrusted to *gogo* laKhanyile and took four days of careful boiling, fermentation, tasting and watching. When it was ready, the beer was transferred to fragile, round, black clay pots and was placed in the Great Hut, where it remained overnight for the ancestors to taste. A goat was slaughtered, skinned and hung next to the brew. Next day, amid much advice and general participation, the goat's head was severed, cleaned and the skull with its elegant horns placed over the doorway of the Great Hut. Then the men hacked the carcass into manageable portions and the cooking began. There was a sense of excitement and anticipation as the air filled with smoke and steam and meaty aromas. This is an occasion when men as well as women do the cooking. Down at the men's enclosure at the cattle *kraal*, they peered anxiously into pots, gauging the progress of their particular assignment.

Make *Shongwe cooking in her outside kitchen; two of her youngest daughters, Mphondi and Welile look on. Concerned about whether the Nestors would like Swazi food, she decided to make maize bread and chicken stew for them.*

Towards midday about thirty neighbours, all relatives, from eight homesteads came to join the family. It was a very hot day. People were pleased when *umkhulu*, now in traditional *lihiya* (a printed cotton cloth tied at his hip) and *lijobo* (a carefully fashioned silver monkey-skin hanging, fore and aft, like a double Highland sporran) called them into the cool, dark shade of the Great Hut to explain to them and to the ancestors that their homestead had been chosen to receive the British visitors. Then he called upon his ancestors, chanting their praise names, and all the people echoed their response in reverend unison:

> *Shongwe!* Shongwe,
> *Mabhengeta!* Mabhengeta,
> *Mncusi, the Lion, the chief!* Mncusi, the Lion, the chief,
> *Descended from laZidze!* descended from laZidze,
> *Descended from Shangase!* descended from Shangase,
> *Shongwe!* Shongwe.

Umkhulu pronounced the final evocative, enigmatic blessing: 'Birds wipe their mouths as they eat. Farewell, ancestors! We shall follow you shortly.' Some beer from one of the clay pots was poured onto the ground, before *umkhulu* himself took a sip from it. The pot was then passed from hand to hand, with each person sipping in turn. The ritual sharing of a specially consecrated drink between the living and departed spirits is as solemn in the Great Hut as it is in a parish church in England.

The meat and maize porridge was distributed to everybody by the daughters-in-law, in a variety of enamelled and china bowls. There was much licking of fingers. Spoons were reserved for the few. The beer was passed around and declared to be very good. The more they drank it, the more they liked it. The young and single congregated behind the buildings, as the young will, to talk and tease and play pop music on somebody's portable radio. The old men disappeared in twos and threes to talk local politics in private corners. The women discussed their children, pregnancies and the rising cost of school books. By dusk everybody had eaten their fill, the daughters-in-law were exhausted and the ancestors, hopefully, had been alerted and placated. The Shongwes went to sleep wondering what they had let themselves in for, but confident that the outcome was now in higher hands.

ଚ ଓ

While the Shongwes brewed, slaughtered and prayed, the Nestors packed and partied. London was bitterly cold. It was fun to walk down the icy pavements to buy sunblock, suntan lotion and mosquito repellent; to dig deep in drawers to find shorts, sandals and bathing costumes; to borrow summer dresses from friends; to be part of the privileged few who would be escaping the northern winter cold for the southern sun. Friends came to congratulate them and envy them and wish

them luck. They brought them cards with printed messages saying Bon Voyage and Good Luck. They all drank wine and got tipsy. Chloe's best friend burst into tears.

The Nestors' televised departure was slow and exhausting. West Norwood to Swaziland took twenty-seven hours – thirteen of them cooped up in an aeroplane. They missed their connection in Johannesburg by minutes and had to wait an extra two hours before making the short, bumpy, fifty-minute flight to Swaziland. It was hot and humid; the sun was shining brightly; the sky was blue. They were in Africa. They were almost too tired to notice or care. They wanted baths, beds, clean clothes. They climbed gratefully into the pick-up and, fighting sleep, drove as fast as they could to the rather glamorous hotel that had been booked for their first night.

ଚ ଓ

The Shongwes had been waiting all day for the Nestors. The missing glass panes from the windows of the porch intended for the English children had finally been measured, bought and puttied into the metal window frame. A new door had been hung in the doorway. The concrete floors had been scrubbed and then polished. They shone like glass. The yard had been swept. *Make* Shongwe, senior among the daughters-in-law, had been up since dawn. She worried about what the British people would like to eat. She remembered her own two weeks in Germany. The worst thing had been the food, all that German food, especially the meat. Well, they called it meat. She knew beef and chicken and goat, but that was none of those. You didn't know what you were eating. She had decided to make maize bread for the English family, and to prepare a chicken stew.

Maize bread is a treat you can only really enjoy in January and February when the maize is still green and full of sap. It was hard work and she had been assisted by Amos's wife, Thandi laMabuza, who had helped her to cut the corn from the cobs with a sharp knife and then to grind it the old-fashioned way, a handful at a time, between two grinding stones, catching the wet pulp on a grass mat. Then the soft, wet ground flesh had been mixed with salt and baking powder and packed back into the maize leaves in small portions, the top of each packet being tied with a shredded leaf. They had boiled the packets of dough in a cauldron for several hours until the bread was ready. The chicken had come as a packet of frozen pieces from the supermarket in Manzini the day before. 'We didn't have a chicken of our own big enough to kill.' Thoroughly thawed in the summer heat, it was then salted, boiled and added to fried onions, green peppers and tomatoes.

One or two curious relatives from neighbouring homesteads joined them, anxious to catch an early sight of the exotic visitors. Everybody was carefully dressed. Mandla, bare-chested save for some beads, was wearing the traditional *lihiya*. The four daughters-in-law were demure in clean wrap-around aprons in the requisite navy or brown Victorian prints, with scarves on their heads. The young daughters, mindful of the latest fashions, wore their best dresses and had oiled their legs and plaited or straightened their hair. The children, who had been dressed in their best, romped and rolled unconcernedly in the red dust. Three-year old Mphondi took off her dress and reverted to her usual naked self.

When the children got hungry they were sent to look for sour porridge left over from the morning meal. 'The bread and chicken are to share with the English people who are coming, to welcome them.'

Because it was a weekday, *umkhulu* was unavoidably away at work. The duties of homestead head therefore devolved to his wife, *gogo* laKhanyile, assisted by *babe* Themba Shongwe, as the heir and oldest male present. He was pensive: 'I am still wondering how the ancestors in this home thought about this, having people from Europe to come and stay with us here.'

                     ᘒ ᘔ

Back at the hotel, the English family was being briefed for its stay. They had all had a good night's sleep. They had chosen their breakfast from a dazzling array of foods. They had swum in the turquoise pool. They had lazed on the green lawns under the palm trees. White-coated waiters had brought them iced drinks.

'This is the kind of Africa I like,' said Lynn. 'It definitely feels like I'm in Africa.'

'I like the vibe,' agreed Robert. 'I'd like to come here for a holiday.'

The children took it all for granted. But now the family had to be prepared for Africa away from the tourist route. They had to understand that theirs was an unusually privileged position. Few outsiders are ever admitted to live in a homestead on Nation Land. The whole community had been consulted, at a chiefs' meeting, and had agreed to their coming. All eyes would be upon them. They would need to conform to local rules, even where these were strange and difficult for them. The people of the homestead would tell them the rules, possibly very gently. 'They won't say: boom, boom, boom, these are the rules. They'll be put across to you – sometimes as a joke, but take them seriously.'

The Nestors should listen carefully to casual hints about their conduct, which might mask a firm instruction. They should take their cues from the behaviour of other people. They should sit down in the presence of their superiors, literally keeping their heads down, as a mark of respect. They should avoid direct eye contact with their elders.

The people of the homestead would treat them as kin. They would look on Robert as a son, a Shongwe, with more privileges than Lynn, who would be regarded as a new daughter-in-law and, as such, an outsider. Each daughter-in-law is an outsider and is subject to three masters: the homestead head, her husband and her husband's mother, her mother-in-law. She is the drudge – kitchen hand, laundry maid, field worker, nursemaid to the many homestead infants, a hewer of wood and a drawer of water. Fortunately this lowly status is always temporary; in the fullness of time she herself will become somebody's dreaded mother-in-law and, as widow, homestead head. Lynn immediately recognized her disadvantaged position. They were all outsiders, but only she was going to be treated as one, and she was not going to stay there long enough to be promoted! 'I'm nowhere, am I, nowhere at all!' All her instincts as a liberated twenty-first-century British woman were aroused: it was a clear case of gender discrimination!

Then the Nestors were stripped of the inessentials in their luggage that would stand between themselves and full participation in the Swazi way of life. The children were the main victims of the purge. Despite their attempts to travel light, they had brought with them the usual Western paraphernalia of toy cars, dolls, cuddly animals, cut-out and pop-up books, story books, colouring books, crayons, felt pens, tennis balls, footballs, inflatable beach balls, playing cards, a compendium of board games, plasticine and two electronic games.

'I want my toys,' sobbed Callum.

'Shush,' said Lynn. 'The Swazi children will share their toys with you, I'm sure they will.'

But the point, of course, was that Swazi children have no toys. If Daniel, Chloe and Callum were to bring all these things with them, they would change the way the Swazi children played – in dozens of clapping, dancing, jumping, chasing and skipping games that need no equipment. The Nestors' toys might make them dissatisfied with a ball made from tightly wrapped plastic bags, a car made from a wheel wired to a piece of bamboo, or an old car tyre steered between two sticks.

'We'll have to make you some toys,' said Lynn to Callum. 'How about that for an idea? You like making stuff. What shall we make?'

'A Gameboy,' said Callum.

Robert and Lynn fared better. Robert kept his skipping rope. 'No, I can't give that up, no way. That is my life, my training. That's what I do to keep fit.' He was contemptuous of the idea that he could skip with a rope made from grass, which he would certainly find at the homestead. 'No way! This is a specially balanced, weighted Italian skipping rope. Just my skipping rope I'm keeping. I can't, I can't leave it. I can't leave my skipping rope. I just cannot leave it.' He doubted that the other men at the homestead, who kept in shape through daily work rather than a work-out, would be as fit as he was. 'If that is the case I will sell my house and move to Swaziland.'

Lynn gave up two mud packs, some sweets, a radio and a book on feng shui, but kept several blockbuster novels, her duty-free cigarettes, Callum's pull-on disposable nappies

and some toilet roll. They were allowed to keep their bath oil, hair conditioner, wet wipes, tissues, after-shave lotion and deodorant.

They also kept copious medical supplies; painkillers, medicines for diarrhoea and vomiting, malaria prophylactics, quinine, antibiotics, an asthma pump, a hypothermia blanket, a mouth-to-mouth resuscitation mask and hypodermic syringes. Lynn had made her position on that clear in London. 'I'll do everything I possibly can to be part of that life over there, but there are some things I'm going to take with me from my life over here. In the event of something dreadful happening, my children will live. I'm quite prepared to do whatever I have to do to fit in, to adapt, but I'm not putting my children's lives at risk. No way. No how. Not for anybody.'

It was decided that the Nestors should start out with as much money in their pockets as a porter at their hotel might expect to earn in a month, roughly £150 (at a rate of exchange of about ten Swazi *emalangeni* to one pound sterling, this was about 1,500 *emalangeni*). In this way they would be no better, but no worse, off than most other households in the homestead. They would be participating as economic equals rather than as privileged Westerners. The Shongwes had been told that they should expect no immediate patronage from their visitors. Only on these difficult terms could the Nestors fully experience contemporary rural African life. The Nestors were warned of the heavy demands that would be made on this small sum. It was January, the beginning of the school term. School fees, books and uniforms would eat into their budget, but, as honorary

On the Shongwe homestead the Nestor children would need to get used to playing with simpler toys than those they were used to at home.

members of the Shongwe homestead, they would never go hungry. They were entering a more communal lifestyle. Other people would share food with them. Robert should think about finding work, like that of the other men of the homestead, in order to pay their way in the weeks to come. Lynn should think about how she might earn money in an informal way, perhaps by selling snacks at the school, by retailing fruit or even by making and selling grass mats, as the other women of the homestead did.

Suitably sobered by the preparations, but optimistic, the Nestors emptied their English purses into a bag for safekeeping for the next ten weeks. Lynn said, 'If this was England, I'd be terrified. We'd be starving. But I know we won't starve here. This is Africa.' Within twenty-four hours they would be the grateful recipients of their first discreet delivery to the homestead of what Lynn called 'proper food'.

ဆ ଓଷ

Swazis have a great sense of occasion. When the Nestors arrived at the homestead, the whole Shongwe clan lined up in rank order beside the Great Hut to shake their hands. As the family clambered nervously out of the pick-up, Chloe and Callum clung to Lynn's hand. Daniel, at thirteen already taller than his mother, stood beside his father in solemn concentration. *Make* Shongwe, speaking in fluent English learnt at work, acted as spokesperson, introducing each member of the homestead by name, position and rank: first the grandmothers, then their sons, then their sons' wives and finally the children.

'This is *gogo* laKhanyile. She is married to *umkhulu*. She is the senior grandmother of this house. This is *gogo* laNkhosi, who is also married to *umkhulu*, who unfortunately cannot be with us. This is Mandla, who is son to *umkhulu*. This is *makoti* laMabuza, who is married to Amos, son of *umkhulu*. Unfortunately Amos is away at work. This is…'

The daughters-in-law were introduced by title and maiden name: marriage among the Swazis does not change a woman's clan. The names went on and on, the welcoming smiles, the three-grip handshakes, the thank yous, the how-do-you-dos, until the very youngest had been introduced.

Then, without further ado, slipping off their shoes at the grass screen, everybody disappeared through the low doorway into the Great Hut, the Nestors among them, and an abrupt silence filled the suddenly deserted yard. The sun was setting behind the mountain. The grey branches of the cattle *kraal* cast sharp shadows across the yard. From the weathered, grass-domed hut, the clear, high voices began to sing, 'Moses, take off your shoes. This place is holy.' Soon *gogo* laKhanyile's voice could be heard in siSwati prayer.

Thank You, God
Thank You, Almighty
Who has saved our lives
Who has seen things inside our lives
Who has seen things we do not know about
Thank You for this white family
You know better why You have decided that we
    should receive them
What did You think of us?
You found our home appropriate
We pray that You help us care for them, talk to
    them nicely.
We pray that we be tolerant of one another
We thank You for having carried them from
    such a far place, by aeroplane and car
We thank You that they have arrived safely in
    this homestead

Because You found us fit to receive the Nestors,
*   please keep them safe while in this homestead*
We pray that we will be able to communicate
*   with one another*
Where we do not understand, we should ask
Where they do not understand, they should ask
We ask You to guide us each day
Help us even with things we have not mentioned
Thank You, Jesus Christ of Nazareth. Amen.

Then, in the perfect harmonies that seem to come naturally to those living in that part of the world, they sang 'I will magnify His holy name'. In characteristic Swazi fashion, the occasion turned secular. The crew standing outside felt excluded when they heard the

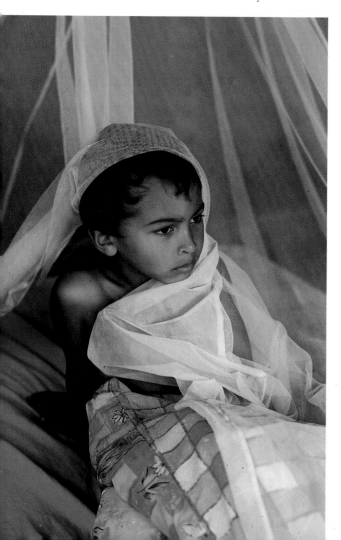

singing turn to dancing, and then uproarious laughter as Daniel gamely joined in. The Nestors had truly arrived.

In the gathering dark they were taken on a quick tour of all the homestead buildings. It was too much to take in. *Babe* Shongwe stood thoughtfully watching the little procession, his wife in the lead.

'What are you thinking?'

'The little ones,' he said, indicating Callum and Chloe, 'I think they are frightened of us.'

Lynn was also a bit frightened. She admitted this later, with a laugh, when everything and everyone had become familiar and predictable; when nobody had got malaria or cholera, or had been accused of witchcraft, or bitten by snakes. Their reception, so well intended and carefully planned by the Shongwes, had been a bit intimidating: all the singing and dancing and clapping in that dark, crowded hut. Apart from *make* Shongwe, you could not understand a word anybody was saying. And all those people, all those names.

When they reached the block-built *rondavel* set aside for them, *make* Shongwe said, 'This is the building for the Nestors.' Then, laying down a rule with a light touch, she continued, '*Babe* Nestor and *make* Nestor are going to stay here. Here in Swaziland we don't allow children to sleep with their mothers, so this is Mum and Dad's room.'

'Oh, it's wonderful!' said Lynn faintly, wondering what was to become of her children.

The 'kids' room', as *make* Shongwe called it, was a thoroughfare – the porch to Mandla's room. Mandla, father of three, is a single man of about thirty-five. It was not an arrangement that British people would have made, but

Callum on his mattress in Mandla's house.

disapproval was out of the question. To the children, *make* Shongwe said, 'This is your bathroom, your candlestick, everything. I hope you'll love this room.' She expected some of her own children to share it with them, and said so, but none of the Nestors heard her.

'It's lovely,' said Lynn again, as the three Nestor children, ignoring the plastic basin, tried to open Mandla's bedroom door in search of the bathroom. They were deftly deflected by *make* Shongwe.

Daniel said stoically, 'We've got a roof, four walls and a door. It's all we need.'

That night, surrounded by their many suitcases, Lynn and Robert slept fitfully on their new, specially purchased double bed in the round house that *babe* Shongwe had built to honour his mother. Their first thought had been to unpack. They had unzipped their bags and pulled possessions out on to the bed. Then Robert said, 'We haven't got no wardrobes', and they zipped them up again. The swift darkness on that first night took them unawares. They fumbled in the dark to find matches, candles, toothbrushes, the children's pyjamas. Robert found the duty-free vodka and went off to share it with the men.

In their separate house nearby Daniel, Chloe and Callum lay down side by side on three new foam mattresses under three new mosquito nets, with a candle burning as a nightlight to stop them from being scared if they woke in the night.

Lynn sat on the bed looking at the tray of strange food that had been put down quietly on the floor, wondering how, when, where and with whom she was meant to eat it. Later she lay awake and worried. She worried about Callum falling head-first into the pit latrine, and about what they were going to eat for breakfast; she worried about how she was going to rinse her hair without running water, and how she was going to survive the next ten weeks.

'It's a bit overwhelming really. I'm not sure what the ground plan is. I'm trying to make sense of everything. Once the novelty's worn off, will it be as appealing? It's all very well to say no electricity, no running water, but when you actually get here... I'm either going to be really, really happy or I'm going to want to go home very shortly. I still really want to do it, but I'm not sure at this moment of time if I can.'

Chloe in bed in Mandla's house.
The mosquito nets proved an unnecessary
precaution; there were no mosquitoes.

CHAPTER FOUR
an unfortunate beginning

It was the start of the school year, a very busy time in every Swazi family. Money has to be found and spent on uniforms, shoes, exercise books, textbooks, school fees and school funds. Absent fathers have to be hunted down by their children and their ex-partners, soliciting contributions. Normal domestic routines are disrupted as mothers have to queue to secure valued places in school for their children, and then queue again at the banks to pay the school fees and funds, which head teachers are otherwise all too often tempted to misappropriate. Children who cannot find places at local schools have to be found lodgings with relatives elsewhere. It is as busy as the ploughing season, but more expensive. Every January the prices of cattle fall at the local abattoirs: supply suddenly exceeds demand as people are forced to convert their wealth into cash.

If Daniel and Chloe were to go to school, they would need to register at eight the very next morning. The nearest school, Zombodze National Primary, was six miles away. To get there in good time for the inevitable queue, the Nestors would need to wake at five o'clock to walk almost two miles to the bus terminus to catch the first bus at seven. It was a challenging prospect for Lynn: 'I never get up before ten to eight at home'. But she had not reckoned on the warm, bright dawn, the Shongwes being up and busy, and Daniel with them, getting bread before five from a bread shop unexpectedly close, up the hillside. It was all very

(opposite)
In the privacy of their room Lynn could be herself rather than make *Nestor. Their specially purchased bed became a focus of the Nestors' domestic life.*

Initially Lynn found all the walking a terrible trial. Locals take it for granted.
Here children walk the last stretch of the road from Ekudzeni to Zombodze.

unfamiliar: dressing from suitcases, using the pit latrine, fetching water from the tap in the yard, washing in cold water in a plastic basin, breakfasting on brown bread and jam, while standing about awkwardly in *make* Shongwe's kitchen, with Callum and Chloe asking where the butter was. Then the walk.

'That walk!' said Lynn later that day. 'I should have known what the walk would be like. We came that way yesterday. It did not sink in that we might have to walk those roads… I hate exercise. I can't stand it. I'm the unfittest person going. This has come as a great shock to my body.'

In London Lynn drives Callum and Chloe to school when it is cold or raining, even though the school is only a hundred yards away, and she fetches Daniel from less than a mile away four times a week. Now they were in a place where all children walk to school by themselves. The two Shongwe children, Cebsile and Xolile, who were showing them the way, walked silently beside them. Cebsile took Callum on to her back.

'I want *you* to carry me,' whined Callum to his mother, but Lynn was having trouble carrying herself. She puffed up the hill, saying that Callum would never be able to do this every day.

'He doesn't have to,' Daniel reminded her. 'Nor do you. I can do this walk easily.' And so he could. He even took turns at helping to carry Callum.

They would have missed the seven o'clock bus had it ever come. As they waited with the other patient passengers in the hot sun for almost an hour, Lynn reflected aloud on the merits of teaching children at home, saying, 'Chloe's never going to manage this.'

The bus that the people from Ekudzeni catch, like all Swazi buses, is privately owned

and run. Buses can be highly lucrative. There is fierce competition for monopolies on routes where the roads are good and the demand is strong. The Ekudzeni route is not one of these. The buses are erratic. They seldom come when it rains and the road is reduced to a slippery mire. The bus owner maximizes returns by giving priority to adult passengers making the long journey to Manzini. Short-haul passengers and half-price children are often left behind. Lynn did not know how lucky she was to be picked up at seven, with her three children. They found themselves squashed on to a shared seat to make space for other fares. Local people, unused to strangers, stared at them.

Lynn found the bus journey threatening. 'I felt vulnerable, the more crowded it got – I didn't even know where we were getting off; even paying on the bus, the strange money, loads of little things.'

By the time she had reached the school, waited around in what seemed a disorderly crowd for ages, queued with other parents of new children and failed to grasp the system for paying school fees, heard Callum say repeatedly that he was tired, hungry and thirsty, and watched Chloe throw up three times, Lynn was ready to give up. School was clearly going to be too much for Chloe. 'I'm not going to send her,' she said to the head-master. 'She's not up to it. It's a very, very long walk and a very long bus journey. It's too much for her.'

She was not sure about registering Daniel, either. The school seemed dirty and disorganized. She could not understand the teachers' unfamiliar accents. She said to Daniel, 'You sure you don't mind coming here? You can manage? You can always pull out again if you don't like it.' But Daniel was game for it and registered for English, maths, religious education, social studies, agriculture, siSwati and home economics. 'Home economics?' queried Lynn.

'We do it with both boys and girls here. We like boys to cook for themselves and learn to manage the house,' said the headmaster. He hoped that Lynn would visit the school frequently to check on Daniel's progress. 'Maybe we are going to learn something from him. If he is a good pupil, we might make him a monitor.'

Daniel was to report the following Tuesday at a quarter to eight, wearing a khaki shirt and trousers and black shoes. He should bring something to eat, or about thirty pence to buy buns, juice and fruit from the hawkers at the school gate. 'But,' said the school secretary comfortingly, 'in February we have a lot of guavas.' Poorer children could pick their lunch for nothing from the fruit growing wild all about the school.

Lynn got 'home' (as, to her surprise, she heard herself call it) feeling hot, exhausted and distressed, and flung herself on to the bed. She could not believe it was only midday. She had been up for seven hours. She wanted to sleep for a fortnight. The journey to school had been a nightmare, but it was not just the school that had upset her. 'I like to think I've done everything. I like to know what I'm doing, and I don't know what I'm doing. I walked into the kitchen this morning. I had absolutely no idea what we were meant to be eating. I'm lost and disorganized. So far supper has appeared, and today lunch appeared and I'm very grateful for it, but what about tomorrow?'

With no thought of tomorrow, Daniel, Chloe and Callum tucked into their delivery of 'emergency food' that the crew had brought them – bananas, Spam, white bread,

mango juice and Smarties – with enthusiasm, leaving their mother to fret.

⁞  

Robert, who had woken before five after a fitful night, had by contrast had a thoroughly enjoyable morning. In borrowed gumboots – a protection against snakes – he had climbed the mountain with Dokta, Themba and Mandla to bring the cattle down. He had spent an hour immersed in the local stream, 'chilling out'. He loved the mountain. 'I feel like I belong in the countryside. I can go up the mountain and sit. I find comfort in my own company.'

He also enjoyed being part of the *esangweni*, the men's enclosure beside the cattle *kraal*. He thought the homestead was 'great, really, really beautiful. I knew people would be really friendly and welcome us. I couldn't have asked for anything better.' The people were 'pleasant, placid, a bit laid back. My kids are totally safe. Everybody in my unit will be OK. It's a once-in-a-lifetime experience.' He thought ten weeks would not be long enough. 'It's going to go quick, too quick.' He was pleased with their accommodation, the soundly built room with its polished concrete floor, the roof of roughly thatched grass. He did not yet know that, like many roofs in the country, it leaked in heavy rain. 'They've gone to so much trouble to make us comfortable. They're not rich.' He had geared himself up to sleeping on a mat on the floor. The double bed was 'a bonus. I thought it would be much more basic'.

He put Lynn's traumatic morning down to her lack of experience. 'It wasn't organized. Lynn's an organized person. As long as she's got a little routine she'll go for it. In a couple of weeks she'll have the school run

sussed. She'll be running down the hill with Daniel and Callum and Chloe. She will. It's a two-hour walk. It's not like West Norwood.' To Lynn herself he said, rather smugly, 'You haven't done what you set out to do. Your responsibilities are sorting out the kids. You've found out there are problems that you have to sort out. You'll do that on Monday. It's a totally different environment from what we're used to.' Robert was full of optimism. He predicted that it would take them a week to 'get into a Swazi routine – or maybe two'.

The Shongwes noticed his enthusiasm and liked him for it. They predicted that, of all the family, he would learn fastest to adapt to Swazi ways. 'He is active, he goes around the homestead and mixes with us. You can see he wants to learn something from us.'

They were less impressed with Lynn. She ignored them; she smoked. Her British holidaymaker style of dress distressed them; she wore shorts all the time. Her bare head showed a lack of propriety in a married woman, signalling to the men that she was unattached and available. She did not share the food that her children seemed always to be eating. If she was to be treated as a daughter-in-law in the homestead, she would have to start behaving like one. But it was not entirely her fault, for she was ignorant. She needed instruction in the rules of the homestead.

The Nestors loved the river which wound its way through the homestead fields. Here Robert 'chills out' with a book.

The thatch on the roof of the Nestors' house leaked badly and needed frequent patching.

This instruction was delivered rather brutally on Lynn's third day on the homestead. It was a Saturday. Robert and Daniel had spent the morning trying to help the Shongwes repair the worn thatch on the Great Hut. It was not a job they understood, nor had they understood what anybody was saying, but the air was warm and the sun was shining. It had seemed pleasant enough, standing around looking willing, or clambering up the crude home-made ladder with armfuls of prepared grass fringes. Swazi thatching is quite unlike British thatching. The British use the thick stalk end of the grass to make a hard surface of bristles. The Swazis use the grass the other way up; the hard grass stalks are carefully laid side by side and then woven with string into a long, mat-like fringe; this is wrapped, layer by layer, around the roof, stalks uppermost until the roof is covered in a cascade of feathery grass ends, like uncombed hair, which is then tied down with a giant grass rope net. It is thinner, softer and more untidy than British thatch, but it lasts remarkably well.

The Great Hut had not been re-thatched since *umkhulu*'s father had built it, twenty-five years before. The women of the homestead had been working hard for months to get ready for this day, cutting the grass up the mountain, drying it and then

Men and women work together tying the thatch to the rafters below.

tying it into great fringes. They had also plaited yards and yards of grass rope to secure the roof. It would be their job to tie the thatch down over the next three weeks. Now they all stood around, admiring their handiwork and watching the men laying the last of the grass on top of the dome. Lynn, dressed in her shorts, was down at the tap, squatting before big plastic tubs of Nestor washing that was soaking. The washing line was heavy with the clothes she had already washed. 'Drip-dry,' she explained to Robert. She was just too hot to wring the clothes.

None of the Nestors had particularly noticed the grey-haired man in overalls who had joined them. None of them had stopped what they were doing to greet him. Was he one of the men employed to look after the cows?

It was *umkhulu*, the most important person on the home-stead, the patron who had given permission for their stay, back home at last from his job in Mbabane. In the early afternoon the Nestors were summoned to the Great Hut to be formally intro-duced to him. Robert had only that morning asked what exactly the Great Hut was for. *Babe* Shongwe's explanation, in halting English, had been brief and to the point, 'It's for people when they come. They have to go inside and be explained how to live.

And when something goes wrong, you have to gather there and sort it out.' Something was already going wrong and was about to be sorted out.

The Nestors crept through the low doorway of the Great Hut into the cool, dark interior smelling of grass. They sat down on the floor, Robert and Daniel to the right with the men, Lynn and Chloe and, after some tearful protest, Callum, to the left with the women. Above their heads rose the dome of tightly latticed saplings. The interior of the Great Hut is in extraordinarily elegant contrast to its ragged exterior. The rest of the homestead were there already, sitting quietly and comfortably on grass mats. They looked on as, formally and gently, *umkhulu* shook each of the Nestors by the hand, politely mouthing each English name in turn and smiling in lieu of the English words. Then, still smiling, he welcomed them, with *make* Shongwe interpreting. He did not know what had brought their two families together, but he trusted God and his ancestors. He hoped they would leave the homestead happy. If anyone was unhappy, the Great Hut was where everything could be thrashed out. Now, he said, their new daughter-in-law would get all the information she needed from the mothers.

Then *make* Shongwe said, '*Make* Nestor, we have something to give you, so the others can go now. This is just for women.' Robert dragged a protesting Callum into the sunshine, leaving Lynn alone, sitting somewhat apprehensively in the gloom with the other women of the homestead.

Wordlessly *gogo* laKhanyile approached her and clumsily wrapped an ankle-length cloth around her waist, covering her bare legs. Still without a word she clumsily dressed Lynn in a long pinafore and wrapped a thick cotton scarf around her head. Then at last she began to speak. 'You are now a daughter-in-law of this homestead, *makoti* Nestor. You are a married woman, so you have to always wear an apron and always cover your head. It is the rule of this homestead.'

It was the first of eight rules for Lynn. Three were simple prohibitions: no trousers, no smoking, no shoes in the Great Hut. One was about sharing food: 'When you cook you give everybody in this homestead food.' One was about the special restrictions on diet that apply to all new daughters-in-law: 'You are not allowed to eat meat or milk from the cows of this homestead, nor eat the eggs from its fowls.'

Lynn was then shown the proper way for women to sit – knees never up, apart or crossed, as British girls are taught at school, but modestly, Swazi-style, with knees together on the ground, preferably straight-legged. *Gogo* laNkhosi demonstrated the preferred posture.

The next rule was about greeting. 'Every day in the morning you must greet everybody. You must say, "How are you, Mother So-and-so?" to everybody in the homestead. And when you go to sleep. It's what we do. That is the daily procedure.' Then, recalling the morning's *faux pas*, she added as an afterthought, 'And at the weekend when *umkhulu* comes, you must say, "Hello, *umkhulu*, how are you?"'

They had one more formality to complete; they were going to give her a child of the homestead to be her own. There was a pause in the proceedings as somebody was despatched to find the child.

As Lynn sat waiting uneasily, somewhat pale and chastised, they said how happy they were that now she was one of the family. They told her how well the apron and scarf suited her, but they did not say it in English and she did not understand them. They assured her that as daughters-in-law they had all been through this procedure themselves.

Then Xolile, *make* Shongwe's sturdy twelve-year-old daughter, arrived. 'This is your new child,' *make* Shongwe said to Lynn. She then turned to her daughter and said, 'Xolile, I am no longer your mum. This is your new mum.' To the nervous laughter of the other women she added, 'You will go to England with your new mum.' She turned to Lynn once more to explain. 'If you want something, you call Xolile. If you want someone to clean your room, you call Xolile. If you want someone to do your washing, you call Xolile. After you have cooked, Xolile will take the food to all the people at home. You can go and fetch firewood with Xolile. You can go and fetch water with Xolile.' Suddenly the session was over. 'Let's go,' she said, and they tumbled out to find their shoes and the sunshine.

It was a routine act of incorporation, the kind of initiation that every new daughter-in-law experiences. Lynn's immediate reaction was outrage. She rushed to the privacy of her room where, to the consternation of her children, she burst into floods of noisy, angry tears. 'It was bad enough before. It's just got twenty times worse.' She sobbed that she had been told to do all sorts of impossible things and that, if she did not do them, they would probably all be kicked off the homestead. Robert was dismayed. They had only just arrived, and he wanted to stay. When he urged calm acceptance of the situation, she snapped back that she did not want a sermon. It was all right for him. He was a man; he could wear what he liked. All her carefully packed summer clothes were suddenly useless. To be forbidden to wear shorts was bad enough. To be forbidden to wear all her

summer skirts was too much. In this hot climate she had to cover herself from top to toe in unflattering, enveloping pinafores and headscarves. It was all too horrible.

Exactly when this dress code emerged as the Swazi norm for married women is unclear. It is strongly reminiscent of the style that white settlers throughout Africa have demanded of their maids for more than a century. Overalls, wrap-around pinafores and cotton caps for domestic workers are still routinely stocked in southern African supermarkets next to the brooms, buckets and scrubbing brushes. It smacks of missionary influence: the narrow range of preferred printed cottons with their charming Victorian designs date from the missionary years when sewing classes, dressmaking and church attendance were first introduced.

This is in clear contradiction to another set of rules for Swazi women's dress. On ceremonial occasions, married Swazi women, particularly those of aristocratic descent, are always bare-headed, their hair teased up in a bouffant style (an effect most easily achieved with a wig made from hair clippings), their temples shaved, a cumbersome, middle-of-the-calf-length black skirt around their waist, once made from black cowhide, now from lightweight synthetics. Nor is it the custom to be prudish about exposed flesh. Women's naked breasts are commonplace at weddings. But for everyday wear, a long wrap-around pinafore of printed cotton has become expected of married women, along with some form of head covering. Outsiders are constantly startled to see women in hats behind computers in government offices. In 1977 the education department made hats compulsory in the classroom for all married women teachers. This regulation was reissued

Ambivalent dress code: the enveloping pinafore and headscarf required of married women stands in stark contrast to the naked breasts and scant skirts prescribed for unmarried girls on ceremonial occasions.

in 2001, to the consternation of Swaziland's modernizers.

For several weeks Lynn did not realize that the prohibition on eating the homestead's meat, milk and eggs applied only to daughters-in-law. She thought it applied to all women. She commented, 'It's a wonder these women don't starve to death.' Rules restricting the social participation of daughters-in-law for their first years in their husbands' homesteads are common throughout Africa. They are often much stricter than those Lynn encountered. Among the Zulu the prohibition extends to several commonplace words, making it hard for brides to talk. *Gogo* laKhanyile recalled her own slow incorporation into the Shongwe household: 'There is a custom that a wife does not eat milk from her in-laws until they give her a cow called *luphakelo*. Even after that my family had to bring a brew to the Shongwes, which was used to bless the milk. Only after that could I drink it.' The restriction on *make* Shongwe has not yet been lifted.

Lynn did not understand the rule about food sharing, either. 'Wasn't there something about cooking for the whole homestead?' she asked nobody in particular. The Swazi homestead pattern, whereby all women cook and each kitchen distributes what it has prepared to every household, was completely alien to her.

Lynn found the rules dreadful, but not shocking. What shocked her was being given somebody else's child. She had clearly heard *make* Shongwe speak those appalling words, 'I am no longer your mum. This is your new mum.' It seemed, to her British ears, a frightening announcement and a responsibility for which she was quite unprepared. British people did not casually give away their children. Children were not commodities. That

was slavery! Had she, a white woman in Africa, just been given a black child slave? She was incoherent with righteous indignation. 'Because everyone else here is black, it's my problem, not theirs.' She did not want a child to order around. 'I've come here to try and fit in, but at the end of the day I'm not African; there are no two ways about it.'

The allocation of Xolile to Lynn had nothing to do with race. Swazis always try to give a new daughter-in-law a daughter of the homestead as her special helper. They are experienced in the ways of the homestead and speed up the newcomer's adjustment to her new home. Lynn had been misled partly by *make* Shongwe's choice of words; Xolile was certainly still *make* Shongwe's daughter. She was also misled by her misunderstanding of what the word 'mother' implies to Swazis. All Swazi children have several people whom they call 'mother'. All their mother's sisters are their mothers, and so are all the many wives of the people they call 'father'. What Lynn was undoubtedly being offered was an extra pair of hands. A twelve-year-old Swazi girl is seen as a useful worker about the home. Lynn was being given first priority on Xolile's time and labour. She took some weeks to come to terms with the idea that children could work, but she never came to terms with the idea that they should work.

Lynn's difficulty with Swazi names and sounds increased her frustration at the injunction to greet everybody by name every day. SiSwati words, with their clicks, are difficult for outsiders to get their tongues round, and there were a lot of people in the homestead to take in. 'I don't even know their sodding names. They all sound the same to me, all "cocoa something".' It was to be several weeks before she mastered the Swazi word for grandmother, *gogo*, the title by which *umkhulu*'s wives are addressed. Happily her version, cocoa, sounded exactly like the Swazi term for great-grandmother, *khokho*, so no one was in the least offended. Lynn groaned, 'I've got to greet all the men! I don't know where to start. I don't know who any of the men are.' Chloe helpfully suggested that she write them down. Lynn was not even sure of the name of the child she had been given. She said to Chloe, 'What's my daughter's name? It begins with a C. Something like Coalie.' They clicked their tongues for a while, searching for the Swazi X sound. Chloe said, 'Ask Daniel. He knows.'

After just three days Daniel knew a lot. When, in the midst of Lynn's outburst, the sound of singing rose from the Great Hut where the women were gathered, Daniel knew they were singing a traditional song to celebrate Lynn's arrival in the homestead as a daughter-in-law. He said, 'Mum! That's a celebration about you!'

'Humph,' snorted Lynn in reply. 'Celebrating my misery.'

When, some minutes later, as her shock and anger hardened into resistance and rebellion and she declared that she was going off the homestead to smoke, it was Daniel who warned her that the mountain was also part of the homestead. She should stick to the public road.

That was exactly what she did. The road was to be her retreat. She had thought about giving up smoking before she left London, but she had decided against it, arguing that she smoked less in hot countries. Besides, there would be no television. 'I might be stressed out at the end of the day. I'd rather have a cigarette than slap my kids.' The homestead's imposition of a no-smoking rule riled her. She decided to curb her public smoking, but she would not stop smoking in private. 'I guess I ought to change my shorts and put a skirt on. What a nightmare!' Thus dressed, she made her way up to the road, with Chloe clinging to her side and suggesting that they run away, back to London, without 'the boys'. Up on the road, Lynn grew calmer. From now on, she said, this would be her favourite spot. 'Up here, having a fag, wearing my shorts. I can take my scarf off as well. I'm Lynn Nestor up here, *make* Nestor down there.'

She had another retreat, in the heart of the homestead: the room they had been given to live in. A room in a Swazi homestead is a private place. Nobody intrudes without an explicit invitation. A room is not usually a place where the homestead rules are broken. The men of the homestead see to that. But, whatever the polite pretence, Lynn was sharing her room with a Nestor, not a Shongwe. As a Westerner, Robert had no more say about what went on there than Lynn herself. Robert found his wife's reaction to the Shongwes' rules deeply disappointing. 'I really thought she was made of stronger stuff. These are the ways that they live. She's not even gonna try and accept it.' But he liked her bare head and her naked legs; he did not mind her smoking, or feeding the children private snacks. They drew the curtains and closed the doors. They discussed getting away from the homestead. Then, accepting the advice Lynn had been given – 'If there's anything you need to know, you just ask' – they went to see *make* Shongwe.

Make Shongwe was reassuring. Things had been much tougher for her when she had first been officially recognized as a daughter-in-law thirteen years ago. She had been involved with *babe* Shongwe for several years and they already had two children. She frequently visited him at the Ekudzeni homestead. It was on one of these occasions that, one morning before dawn, the Shongwe elders had seized her from beside Themba, had taken her into the cattle *kraal* and smeared her with red ochre. This is the *teka* marriage ritual. By using red ochre, the Shongwes had appropriated her as a daughter-in-law. She had been forbidden not only the milk, meat and eggs that Lynn had been forbidden; she had not been allowed to sit on a chair. She had been expected to work so hard that she used to take aspirin for the pain. At that time the homestead had no tapped water. It all had to be fetched from the stream in buckets balanced on the head, which was heavy work. She had wanted to wear a hat to cover her head, but the homestead had insisted on heavy cotton headscarves. Fortunately *make* Shongwe had a well-paid job near her mother's home, so she stayed there most of the time, visiting Ekudzeni only at weekends.

She had only recently given up her job and come to live permanently at Ekudzeni. The Shongwes' was a far stricter homestead than the one she had grown up in. Now she was used to it. In some homesteads, she said, married women were allowed to wear trousers. Her daughters would probably have a much easier time when they married. It was a rueful prediction.

'It's not our Swazi way,' she told the Nestors, but if they wanted to get away for a day – to smoke, to wear what they liked, to buy familiar food – then her son Senzo, who was home for the holidays, would show them the way to the nearest town.

Daniel taking a shower at the men's enclosure at the cattle kraal.

CHAPTER FIVE
'proper food'

Robert had predicted that it would take them a week, maybe two, to get into what he called 'a Swazi routine'. The routine they got into was rather different from that prevailing among the households of the other daughters-in-law. Chloe's vomiting was the catalyst. She and Callum, accustomed to pick and choose and snack, as many English children do, refused to eat the unfamiliar, stodgy food that the Shongwes cooked. Even in London, Callum and Chloe are finicky eaters. 'Callum won't eat dinner. Never eats dinner. He's in and out of the fridge, a perpetual snacker. Chloe's much the same,' said Lynn. They also eat out at local fast-food outlets. 'Callum's at home in McDonald's. Burger and chips, or a piece of chicken and chips, and a Coke. That's quite a nice treat for him.' For two days the children squabbled over the dwindling supplies of boxed fruit juices and sliced white bread, provided by the crew to minimize the culture shock.

ဆ ಛ

(opposite)
Callum has some
'proper food'.

On their fourth day in the country, confined by the restrictions that had been placed on Lynn, and yearning for the familiar, the Nestors took up *make* Shongwe's offer and made their way by foot and ramshackle bus to the nearest town, Manzini. There, at the bus terminus, on vinyl, chrome and plastic chairs, to the beat of last year's top of the pops and the revving of fifty diesel engines, they

Money is an integral part of rural Swazi life. Everybody buys some food. At the wholesale vegetable market at Manzini women stock their local wayside stalls.

ordered chicken and rice and Coca-Cola and spent at one sitting half as much as a Shongwe household spends on food in a week.

They went to Manzini again the following day, to buy Daniel's school uniform, and, weighed down with *make* Shongwe's shopping order, came home in a taxi. They went again before the week was up. Their allowance of local currency was dwindling at the speed of light, but they had two fall-back positions: Lynn had negotiated the postponement of Daniel's school fees for six weeks, and she had 'a bit put aside'. Paradoxically, the Shongwes acquiesced, and even collaborated, in these escapes. They thought it silly, unnecessary and extravagant, but the Nestors were foreigners. Allowances had to be made.

Manzini is Swaziland's fastest-growing town with a population of approximately 100,000 at the beginning of 2000. It's a hot, busy, bustling place, with dirty cracked pavements thronged with down-at-heel shoppers from the countryside, and gutters full of dropped drinks cans and polystyrene plates stained with takeaway foods. Until very recently it was spurned by all but the cheapest of the chainstores that lock southern Africa's small towns into boring clones of one another. Portuguese, Greek and Indian traders used to monopolize its few trading stores. Now the bigger regional stores have opened branches in a noisy shopping mall with an underground car park. On the edge of town there's a shopping centre with an Italian restaurant, a fountain and a cinema. But there are still weeds growing between the paving stones, and coops of thirsty hens for sale on the pavements. On undeveloped plots, cannas and frangipanis flower, and hawkers set up makeshift stalls under fruiting banana and pawpaw trees. The streets are noisy with jammed traffic. Women with babies tied to their backs and loaded shopping bags balanced on their heads move like dancers through the crowds.

The Manzini handicraft market has become a major centre for regional trade in all the hand-produced goods that rural people without wage income make and sell for cash. Very early on weekday mornings the streets around the market are crowded with vehicles and people bringing and buying stock. Traders from Johannesburg come with empty pick-ups. Traders from Mozambique come laden with sculptures and dyed cloths from the north and, from the south, painted masks, mortars and pestles, small-scale wooden replicas of popular cars and buses, carved birds, drums, seed necklaces, decorated dishes and colourful, crude oil paintings. From Swazi homesteads women come carrying bundles of grass floor mats, sleeping mats and table mats, laundry baskets and wastepaper baskets, mats woven from old plastic bags, bowls made from telephone wire and traditional clay pots. Men bring sacks of carved dishes, and hundreds of identical carved soapstone elephants, hippopotamuses and busts of old men.

With few exceptions, these are items that nobody uses – neither the makers in remote rural places nor the consumers. They are for the tourist trade, and are carried by middlemen (who are mostly middle-women) to the places where tourists congregate. The better-informed, better-organized traders make their way by train, bus and pick-up to Cape Town and Durban, Johannesburg and the Kruger National Park. Others walk the white South African suburbs bartering these curios for cast-off clothes. This is a laborious trade plied by women. The resale value of the clothes is high, but only those with kin in South Africa – whose houses serve as depots for the piles of old dresses, coats and shoes – manage it successfully. Second-hand clothes are a major item at Manzini market, but there is much else besides: raw and cooked food, livestock, watches, trinkets, traditional medicines, traditional dress. Some traders offer services like haircutting, watch-mending, dressmaking, tailoring, shoe repairs and the framing of anything from primary-school certificates and family photographs to lurid reproductions of the Virgin Mary, politicians, the king and his mother, Nelson Mandela and the national football team.

The Nestors' reaction to Manzini was blasé. 'It's a city, same as any other city. There's loads of nice shops. There's nice jewellers and nice clothes shops.' But what Lynn liked about Manzini was that it wasn't the homestead. 'It's a bit more normal to me and it gets me off the homestead. This is the only thing. My life here is not much different to my life at home: I'm washing, I'm cooking, I'm cleaning, I'm looking after the children. I do all that at home. The difference is that I'm stuck here. I'm a sociable person. This is why I like Manzini. There's people around me, different people. Even if I don't speak to them, I like sitting and watching people, listening to conversations. It makes me – like

I say, it breaks up the day. I come back feeling a different person.'

In town Lynn could take off her horrid pinny and headscarf. She could bare her legs and be herself. Initially they were disappointed not to find a tourist information centre. 'I don't think there's much to help you out, if you're a tourist.' But they did find an internet café and opened an account. Lynn was exuberant. 'One pound for half an hour. Cheaper than phone calls. Contact with the outside world again! I can't wait to go back and see who's sent me one back.' They did not wait long.

At first the Shongwes observed the Nestors' addiction to Manzini with detachment. They insisted only that they be informed about it. This was another rule of the homestead. People arriving and leaving the homestead had to report to the head – it was their custom. The Nestors duly reported. The Shongwes marvelled at how often they reported. *Make* Shongwe said, 'They have to keep going to town every now and then, yet town is very far. We don't have any shops near us. I think they have a problem with that. They like going to town. They like going there, there, there. The best thing would be for them to have a car. They keep calling taxis, taxis. It's expensive actually.'

Lynn blamed the children, claiming that they were 'really bored'; it was good to get them off the homestead. She had found a small park with a swing and a slide. 'It breaks the monotony of being here. It's something to look forward to, despite the long walk and the bus ride.' But it was expensive. Soon all they would be able to afford would be the bus fare and a drink. She said, 'I hope Robert gets a job soon so that we can go every week.'

At the end of their first fortnight Robert observed, 'We don't try to be Swazis when we're not.' It was a significant statement. They were outsiders, participating in the homestead from the edge. They were not trying to be assimilated. They wore distinctive clothes. Unlike all the other men, Robert wore shorts. He went job-hunting dressed exotically in shorts, a baseball cap and sunglasses. Ever since black men in southern Africa were required to wear short trousers as domestic servants and were addressed as 'Boy', they have spurned shorts, which are also the standard dress for a certain rugged outdoor type of white man. Only the most sophisticated

Swazis, who have lived abroad and absorbed another dress code, affect this white-man-in-Africa dress.

On the other hand, Daniel, unlike most of the other schoolboys, never wore shorts to school. Unlike the other young girls, Chloe seldom wore a dress. To the Shongwes' amazement she always had her flat, child's breasts covered, even when she went swimming in the river. Swazis are very free with naked breasts; girls on the Shongwe homestead are casual about buttoning the fronts of their dresses.

'What is wrong with the child's breasts that she covers them?' asked *gogo* laKhanyile on the Nestors' first day in the homestead, when Chloe appeared in her bikini.

'It is their custom,' said *make* Shongwe knowledgeably. 'They think the breast should always be covered.'

The Nestors persisted in wearing white shirts and socks every day, despite the penetrating red mud. Their socks hung exotically by the score on the washing line each day. On wet days they festooned the inside walls of their room, hanging from nail to nail on sagging pieces of string. They gave rise to an enormous amount of rubbing and scrubbing. Nobody else on the homestead wore socks. But the Nestors were not Swazis; they had their

Being different. The Nestor's socks hung on the washing line by the stove everyday.

(opposite)
British modesty. Chloe never adopted the bare-breasted style of Swazi girls.

own standards to maintain. They were not going native. Only Lynn, in her compulsory long skirts and headscarf, looked inconspicuous on the homestead. As she gradually evaded this rule, she too looked more and more exotic, with the enveloping headscarf gradually reduced to a narrow headband. She was, as she said, being herself.

She bought herself a thermos flask and spent her first week developing a strategy for filling it with hot water. It was challenging to organize even the familiar flow of instant coffee, without an electric kettle. 'There are pots full of boiling water first thing in the morning, but by the time I've got the coffee and gone back to get the water, it's been shoved off to put the maize on and I've just missed it.' Daniel quickly learnt to light the fire for her and bring her hot water. After a fortnight Lynn said, 'I'm getting a bit more confident about going out there and getting water when I feel like it. Before, I was waiting for other people to do it.'

Despite their continuing access to familiar fast food, the children seemed to be losing weight. Lynn became anxious. 'I knew Callum had lost weight when I went to pick him up. He was as light as a feather. That triggered alarm bells.' When, a week later, they were all weighed as part of their routine medical examination for visa purposes, Lynn confirmed the children's weight loss. 'Chloe's lost a stone, Callum's lost nearly three-quarters of a stone, Daniel's lost a stone.'

Two days later, when Chloe vomited again, Lynn used her emergency phone: Chloe needed to be seen by a doctor. He prescribed a routine antibiotic and suggested blood tests for a thorough diagnosis, both of which Lynn declined. 'I think it's the antimalarials myself. That and homesickness.

She's missing her friends. So I'm stopping the malaria medicine and I'll see how it goes.'

The medical panic had served a different end. 'I've had to renegotiate the food situation,' Lynn said. 'So we've been to the supermarket and they're going to be eating proper food – that's wrong, isn't it, it's not politically correct – our sort of food from now on.' She bought baked beans and instant noodles. 'Just stuff I can cook quickly and not interfere with what everybody else is doing.' Besides fruit and carrots, she bought familiar packaged breakfast cereals, peanut butter, fruit juice, flavoured milk and white bread. 'They won't eat the bread here because it's brown. I don't buy brown bread at home. We stick to white.' This kind of food is well beyond the rural Swazi budget, but it was an emergency; the crew was paying.

Within their first week the Nestors had made an important decision about the children. 'I'm definitely not making them lead the Swazi rural life.' Lynn declared that she felt a bit guilty for trying to make them eat the homestead food at all. 'It probably wasn't the best idea.' This decision had significant implications. The Nestors were stepping outside the set of rules for food sharing that binds the discrete parts of a homestead together. The decision set the Nestor children apart, but it also set Lynn apart. From now on she was tied to a different regime from the other women. They cooked together for the whole homestead; she cooked privately for her own children. She really was too busy with her own children to attend to the rest of the homestead.

ಬ ಛ

In the rural African experience, food is worlds away from the pre-cooked flavoured noodles and the tinned beans that Lynn

proposed to 'slip on quickly' for her children. Food is something wrested from unrefined ingredients usually grown by the homesteaders themselves. The Swazi staple, formerly millet, is now maize. Once grown and harvested, the crop has to be laboriously transformed into food. It has to be dried, shelled, cleaned, ground – and then cooked. All this is women's work. They cook twice a day, in the mornings and again in the late afternoon. They are responsible for making sure that the food is there – if not from their own stores, then purchased. Extra ingredients, to add to the daily staples of home-grown maize, pumpkins and beans, may have to be bought. Each woman must supply these from her own purse. Women acquire these skills as girls, from their mothers or grandmothers. As new wives, they serve a further apprenticeship by being attached to a senior woman's kitchen until they are sufficiently mature to warrant the independence of their own kitchen.

Daughters-in-law usually go into town once a month to buy salt, cooking soda, stock cubes and stock powder, and, for a treat, rice and a packet of frozen chicken pieces: heads and feet are the cheapest cuts and make a tasty sauce. Swazis also eat chicken tripe and offal. If the homestead gardens are empty, they may

Thandi laMabuza stripping maize cobs outside her borrowed kitchen. In the background, left, is the house she shares with Amos; and to her right, her own dilapidated kitchen, showing typical construction: stones supported by a wooden frame are plastered with mud.

also buy onions and tinned tomatoes, green peppers and pumpkin leaves in season. Thandi laMabuza said, 'I go once a month. I buy enough for the whole month, but when it's finished I give money to people going to town so they can purchase that for me.' The demands on the women, as cooks, fluctuate with the flow of people to and from the homestead.

In the mornings, when they first wake, they usually eat sour porridge, *incwancwa*. This is made from fermented maize meal that has been steeped in warm water for at least twenty-four hours. The fermentation adds nutritional value. The porridge is eaten hot, sometimes with sugar. For a treat, about once a week they have brown bread and sweet, milky tea instead. *Make* Shongwe remarked, 'That is an expensive meal: sugar, bread, tea and milk. We don't have the money. It's better to do sour porridge.' At the weekend, when *umkhulu* is home, instead of *incwancwa* they serve *mahewu*, his favourite: a cold drink made from very thin, slightly sweetened maize porridge, which has been allowed to ferment for at least a day.

The basis of the Swazi evening meal is a much stiffer, unfermented maize-meal porridge, which can be cooked to a soft consistency with a lot of water *(lipalishi)* or to something stiff and solid, very like Italian polenta *(liphutfu),* cooked with just a little water. About once a week this is eaten with a chicken stew. On most days maize is eaten with a vegetable sauce made from any easily grown green leaf, such as spinach or pumpkin leaves, or from the wild plants *ncuncuza*, *imbuya* and *ligusha* that spring up, unbidden

All outside cooking is done in cast-iron three-legged cauldrons.

but welcome, in the fields. Thandi laMabuza exaggerates when she says, 'We are in the rural areas where we are starving, so we always eat *ligusha*', but this is a popular Shongwe food: cheap and tasty. The leaves are boiled for a few minutes with cooking soda (to retain the green colour). Fried chopped onions and green peppers can be added, or stock cubes if you have them. The mixture is then vigorously stirred 'until the leaves are destroyed'.

Not all Swazi cooking is simple and bland. Take *bubedze*, which the Shongwes prepare when a goat is slaughtered. First, you skim the blood from the various pots of boiling meat. It is a dull reddish-brown, with the consistency of curd cheese. Then you press the paste between traditional grinding stones until it is smooth, like plasticine. You put the

paste in an enamel dish and add to it stock from one of the boiling pots. It thickens into a brick-coloured sauce. The cooking now transfers from the women to the men. The dish is carried to the men's fire, where the chopped liver and tripe are already simmering in one of several pots. In a clean, small pot some fat is rendered down, and the blood mixture is added to this, together with some pieces of liver and tripe. Uncooked blood, saved from the butchering, is then added. The mixture simmers for several hours before being served warm, as a thick sauce. The taste – though not the texture – is not unlike that of English black pudding. Like black pudding, *bubedze* is not a particularly popular dish with the young.

Whatever the women in each kitchen prepare must be shared, not just with one household but with whoever else happens to be at home. In each kitchen the food is judiciously served into a number of bowls, one for each group of people eating together, and then carried from house to house. In a large homestead like the Shongwes', with three kitchens currently in use, this ensures some variety – though of a completely unplanned kind. Monotony is not seen as a problem among people where the food supply itself is precarious. Asked whether she ever enquires what the others are cooking on a particular day, Thandi laMabuza says, 'I do not ask. It does happen that we all cook the same food, because we don't know who is cooking what. You only know what another is cooking if you happen to visit her kitchen. If you notice that she has cooked *ligusha* then you can change.'

Once they are old enough to fend for themselves, Swazi children eat apart from their mothers, from a communal plate. As households share, so do people. Sharing is implicit in all the arrangements. Children do not need to be instructed to share. Toddlers, given a cup of something to drink, will sip and pass it on. School children, with money to spend at the food stalls set up by their mothers in the playground, expect to divide their purchases – a banana, an avocado, a packet of crisps, a fried fish head – among their friends. People will pass a toasted or boiled maize cob around; everybody takes a row, removing the seeds expertly with their thumb, rather than with their teeth as the English eat it.

In this culture of food sharing, the Nestors' policy of giving special food to their children jarred. Chloe and Callum would appear in their doorway at all hours drinking cups of milk, chewing apples, sucking with straws at boxes of fruit juice. *Gogo* laKhanyile observed all this and reserved judgement. 'I am still not in a position to say whether they are bad or good people. I am still observing and studying them.' They had not yet impressed her with their generosity. 'If I was to see them give out something, I would be in a position to say, "Yes, they give," But as of now, there is nothing I can produce to substantiate that statement.'

Lynn and Robert resolved that, together with Daniel, they would eat with the Shongwes 'as much as possible'. Their private supply of familiar children's foods made that decision easier, for in emergencies there was always bread and peanut butter to fall back on. Lynn said that this was not cheating. She saw other women eating snacks in their kitchens. As a new daughter-in-law, Lynn had been assigned to cook with *make* Shongwe. Thandi laMabuza had earned her own kitchen, but *gogo* laKhanyile still had the wives of two of her sons cooking with her. The

Make *Shongwe stirs sour maize porridge,* incwanca, *at her outside fire.*

fourth kitchen in the homestead once belonged to *gogo* laBhembe, but she had moved away.

Make Shongwe has a substantial kitchen with a corrugated iron roof and a cast-iron wood-burning stove, which is not often lit, since it is cheaper and easier to cook on an open fire. Provided it is not raining, *make* Shongwe does her cooking in three-legged cauldrons just outside her kitchen door, on a fire laid on a sheet of corrugated iron, protected by a windbreak of stacked concrete blocks. She says she envies *gogo* laKhanyile and Thandi laMabuza their old-fashioned kitchens, built of mud under thatch; when it rains they can still make a fire on the floor in the middle of the room. The smoke drifts through the roof: there are no chimneys. When it rains hard, *make* Shongwe's outdoor fireplace is impractical. She has to retreat to the indoor kitchen, where some foodstuffs and all her cooking utensils are stored, and there light the wood stove, portable gas stove or paraffin burner. The outside fire burns wood gathered for nothing on the mountain. The wood stove needs heavier logs, which have to be sawn. Gas and paraffin

– quicker to use and more convenient – are the most expensive fuel of all. Wood is still the main source of fuel for 60 per cent of Swazi households.

Although the Shongwes cook only twice a day, people who feel hungry at midday can always find cold food left over from that morning. As a new daughter-in-law, Lynn was expected to assist *make* Shongwe at both the daily cooking sessions. Indifferent to these expectations, she allocated herself two afternoon sessions a week and anticipated exclusive responsibility for these times. 'I like a routine. I said to *make* Shongwe, "Could I just do dinners on Wednesdays and Thursdays?"'

Lynn was trying to impose her own version of order on to the seemingly haphazard Swazi approach to the preparation of meals. She wanted her duties to be well defined and limited. She needed a roster. Not for her the tiresomely vague obligation to help *make* Shongwe fourteen times a week. She wanted a piece of turf of her own to control. Her own house and offspring came first. In this way she could ensure that at least twice a week her children would eat with the homestead. She would cook things they liked. She argued that this arrangement was reasonably fair, given the small size of her family and the fact that she would have to be cooking for her children every other night as well, observing, 'That's my logic and it seems to be quite acceptable.'

It was not. After a month *make* Shongwe expressed frank disappointment in Lynn. She had expected the Nestors to be 'more like us… but the mother, no. She is like somebody else. She doesn't want to be involved… When we are cooking she doesn't want to join in the cooking, like we are doing. She only cooks twice a week. Like now, what she likes is just to sit where she is, just in the house with the kids, or rather sleeping. We are thinking it's about time she learns more.'

To the contrary, Lynn was thinking that she'd already gone too far in accommodating an alien culture. 'When I first got here I was so overwhelmed by the whole thing. I was scared. I was very nervous about upsetting people and the right way to go about things. Instead of being myself, I was trying to be what everybody else wanted me to be, which is ridiculous, because I can't be anything other than myself.'

ഇ ൽ

From the start, the Shongwes had worried about whether or not the British would find their food palatable. The evening meal in the Nestor household in London is, above all, a quick affair. Lynn describes her usual routine. 'If it's a normal working day, then it'll be spaghetti on toast, or pasta. I do a lot of pasta, because it's quick… I do a lot of stuff with rice as well, because it's nice and quick. Robert trains three nights a week, so I don't cook for him. He gets a takeaway, because he doesn't get in till ten o'clock and I'm not going to start cooking again then.'

Robert takes this opportunity to eat more diversely than Lynn and the children: fish and chips, curry, Chinese and West Indian, which he describes as 'similar to what we get here, but the main ingredient is rice; here, instead, theirs is based around maize'.

The Shongwes anxiously examined the Nestors' returned food tray to see what they had eaten and what they had left. *Gogo* laKhanyile said, 'I think they will get used to it. They are willing to learn, because they eat. I think they like a maize cob, the roast one.' Daniel did, indeed, rapidly acquire a taste for toasted and boiled maize cob; even Callum came to eat it after a month. Lynn, however, compared it unfavourably with the much sweeter corn on the cob that they ate in London. 'Here I hate it. It's got no taste.'

But none of them got used to the daily diet of bland, boiled maize meal. Robert said, 'How can I tell you what it tastes like? It tastes of nothing.' Even more unpalatable to them than the maize was *ligusha,* which Lynn called 'the green slimy stuff'. She said, 'How can I put this delicately? I can't. It's got the consistency of snot, basically. It looks like it; it feels like it. You can't pick it up on the spoon, it's so slimy. It's just the grossest thing I've ever come across. It's vile.'

However, they liked another Swazi staple, boiled dried beans, which they called 'bean casserole'. They also liked pumpkin, and what they termed 'bubble and squeak' – shredded, steamed onions and cabbage. After ten days in the homestead Robert said, 'That's as much as I can take. The rest of it, I don't like.' But, like it or not, he bravely ate it, especially when he was with the other men at the cattle *kraal.* After one or two jocular attempts to organize eating in the Western way ('Where's the plates?' 'She didn't bring no knives and forks!'), he learnt to dip his fingers into the communal dishes. 'With my constitution,' he said, 'I can take it.'

Lynn quickly established her menu for the two nights she was in charge of the kitchen. On Wednesdays she cooked rice with tinned pilchards, and on Thursdays chips with scrambled eggs. The Shongwes all liked Wednesday's rice and pilchards. *Babe* Shongwe declared it 'number one' when he first tasted Lynn's version of it. Rice is a luxury in Swaziland, for in comparison with maize, it is very expensive. People who put on airs and attempt to rise above their station are described as 'people who eat rice every day'. Chips are a novelty, from the new fast-food chains that are shackling Swaziland to the global market. When Lynn was told by some of the girls that chips were their favourite food, it seemed appropriate that she should show them how easily they could be made at home. She prided herself on the skill with which she could cut a bucketful. '*Make* Shongwe thinks I've got a chip cutter in my room.'

It was perfectly true that the Shongwe children loved chips. They adored them the first time Lynn made them. They loved them the second time. But as week followed week, chips on Thursdays seemed less and less of a treat. The adults were frankly tired of them. The chips were no substitute for what the Shongwes thought of as 'proper food': maize meal in one of its many forms. In the fifth week of the Nestors' stay, *babe* Shongwe and *umkhulu* complained about the chips, through *make* Shongwe. It was a typical Swazi complaint, indirect but persistent. *Make* Shongwe said to Lynn and Daniel (who loved to assist in the cooking), '*Umkhulu* is hungry. He is saying, "Chips with what?"'

'Chips with egg,' said Daniel, thinking of Norwood High Street.

'I wonder how *umkhulu* will survive on that?' said *make* Shongwe. She tried again, '*Make* Nestor, there is sour porridge left. Let me prepare it for *babe* Shongwe, because he is complaining that he is hungry.' This she duly did. Lynn said that *she* had no intention of cooking maize for supper.

Food remained a difficult topic throughout the Nestors' stay. They seized every opportunity to buy familiar snacks whenever they were away from the homestead. At the beginning of March the worsening outbreak of cholera in Swaziland came as a mixed blessing

for the Nestors. At first the epidemic had been confined to the south of the country, close to the part of South Africa that was initially affected. Then it moved into the Manzini region. It was not a particularly virulent strain, and the death rate was low, but when *babe* Shongwe's sister apparently succumbed to it, the funeral took place at the Shongwe homestead.

Lynn commented, 'People from her homestead, where cholera is rampant, will be coming here, eating, drinking. The risk is now very real. We're not going to eat the homestead food any more, or drink their water.' It was the perfect diplomatic excuse for ending what had always been one of the more difficult aspects of their relationship with the homestead. Thandi laMabuza lent them a paraffin stove. They could finally openly bring in their own supplies of Western food and bottled water. They cooked in their room; they did not share their food.

Paradoxically, despite this withdrawal from the homestead's food-sharing practice, the funeral was to prove the turning point in their relationship with the Shongwes. It was after this that the Nestors at last became closer to them.

The Nestors' special food needs made for a chronically overcrowded room.

CHAPTER SIX
living off the land

Like most rural homesteads, the Shongwes try to produce all their own food. Fields are carefully allocated to each household within the homestead, according to the availability of labour and the number of mouths to be fed. Much of the agricultural work is done communally, first on one household's fields, then on another's. As in all homesteads, everybody has to give priority to the fields set aside in the name of the deceased grandmother. These fields belong to the Great Hut, which is also dedicated to her. The produce from grandmother's fields serves as a shared food reserve for the homestead, and is controlled by her son, *umkhulu*.

By the time the Nestors arrived in the homestead in mid-January, the fields had already been ploughed and the maize sown. In *make* Shongwe's words, 'We are about to close down what we are doing now, but we are going to plant beans at the end of January.' The Nestors missed the special prayers to the ancestors for the protection of the crops. Themba said, 'We normally prepare a brew for the ancestors, prepared from maize kept from the previous season. We inform them that we are about to start planting the maize, and we do not know whether we are going to have a good harvest, or whether we will not have enough.'

The Shongwes' agricultural practices are as traditional as their religion. Everybody helps to grow the maize. The absent sons send money from their wages to make sure that the land

(opposite)
Lynn in babe *Shongwe's vegetable garden.*

Annual leave. Babe *Shongwe, in casual contemporary traditional dress*
of synthetic leopard print, attends to his household's irrigated vegetable garden.

is both ploughed and fertilized, but the Shongwes require less money for this than most Swazis, because they have enough cattle – about forty – to provide their own oxen for most of the ploughing. Since ploughing takes place at the end of the dry winter, when grazing is at its poorest and oxen tire quickly, only people with a large herd are likely to have adequate draught-power. Others have to hire tractors, plough with cows and donkeys, or borrow oxen from their neighbours. The problem is that everybody wants to plough at the same time, when the rains have first softened the soil. Only the lucky few – those who own their own traction – can plough and plant at the optimum moment. The poorest people turn the soil using hoes. If the rain comes late, as it did in 2000, the Shongwes, being pushed for time, have to hire a tractor to help them. This is a very costly business: they paid almost ten pounds an hour, spending as much in one hour as one of their daughters, a factory worker in Matsapha, earns in a week. Once you start hiring a tractor, careful calculation is necessary lest the cost of growing maize exceeds the alternative cost of buying it.

The capricious rainfall is every peasant's bane. The Shongwes have been able to minimize its impact by piping water, which is fed by gravity, from the nearby mountain stream to two sprinklers. In two fields at least their 'rain' now falls predictably. They are able to start planting as early as August, ahead of the first rains in September. In past decades, the timing of ploughing and the planting of crops was centrally controlled by the king. In some chiefdoms people still have to await a signal from their chief that the ploughing season has started. This is because all the cattle in a chiefdom are, by custom, allowed free range during the agriculturally slack winter months to graze on the stubble from the previous season. Those without cattle benefit from the fertilizer casually dropped by other people's foraging cattle. But once somebody starts cultivating their fields, the cattle must be restricted once more to the communal grazing lands, lest they eat the new shoots. The Shongwes get away with early ploughing by fencing some fields. This is another contentious new issue, for fencing runs counter to the ethos of communalism that has shaped past farming practices.

Fertilizers are an expensive item in most Swazi budgets. The Shongwes are able to save money by using the dung from their cattle, rather than the chemical fertilizers recommended by the government, but this is hard work – men's work. The dung has to be dug out from the cattle *kraal* during the dry winter months, loaded on to wheelbarrows and pushed down the steep slopes to the fields below, where it must be spread, using a hoe or shovel, before being ploughed in. Robert Nestor missed this vigorous task.

The Shongwes also supply their own seed by saving their choicest maize cobs each year, to use the following year. Other homesteads buy newer, faster hybrid varieties, which the government recommends, but the Shongwes prefer what they call 'Swazi' maize. It is stronger, tastes better and, above all, keeps longer.

Once the plants are established – in mid-October on the Shongwes' irrigated fields, later in rain-fed fields – the back-breaking work of weeding begins. Although each row of maize needs to be weeded only once, the fields are large and the weeds easily outstrip the young maize plants. When children are big and strong enough, they share this task, working before school in the morning and at weekends. People rise at first light and work for two or three hours before the sun overhead is too hot. The Nestors arrived just in time to help with the last of the weeding. Lynn was quickly conscripted, 'But first,' said *make* Shongwe, 'you need a proper apron to work in and gumboots so that you don't get bitten by snakes.'

The clothing issue continued to be a great source of irritation to Lynn. She resented the sheer volume of clothing she was expected to wear in the hot climate, and the unnecessary drain on their limited cash resources. In ill humour, she allowed herself to be taken to Manzini to buy her apron and gumboots. 'You look lovely!' the dressmaker said as Lynn put on the cheapest apron on the rail. 'Now you are no longer *make* Nestor; you too are *make* Shongwe!' It was cold comfort. What she wanted was to be Lynn Nestor, a free agent, a self-determining individual, whose behaviour was guided by her own will and intelligence, not by a set of rules imposed upon her.

She found it surprisingly pleasant to be working in the fields the next day, as the sun came up. She thought of herself as a very poor gardener. 'I'm not famed for my green fingers. Even grass dies in my garden. I'm the girl who can kill grass.' But hoeing out the weeds was satisfying. 'You can see the results immediately.' She slowly mastered the rhythm of the hoe. It was relaxing.

The maize field, with its weeds, formed the common ground that she had found so hard to establish with the Shongwes. They began to talk to one another. They discussed how much money you needed every month if you were growing all your own food. The Shongwes needed about sixty to eighty pounds a month. Lynn was impressed at their economy. She said, 'There's an awful lot of

The Good Life going on here.' They talked about what you did if you did not have enough money. Lynn told them about her social network in London, how they would 'help each other with a tenner' at the end of the month if they ran short. She said, 'It's quite a good little system – like a homestead, but we don't grow any food.'

They talked about employment. Robert was going to have to look for work. *Make* Shongwe warned that this was likely to be frustrating: there were few jobs available. In her opinion it was better to rely on the fields. 'Going to Johannesburg to look for work is a waste of time. Banging on somebody's door, and on all the doors it's written "No Vacancy", and the kids are starving. You have to grow a garden.'

They talked about deferred payment of school fees. Lynn was relieved to hear that the Shongwes had not paid theirs either. When, at eight-thirty, it was time to stop, Lynn said, 'Let's start earlier tomorrow. I could weed the whole field by myself.' But the weeding season was almost over. Although the Shongwes returned to the fields several times, Lynn weeded only once more.

Maize takes six months to grow, but in the fourth month it is ready to eat green. It can be boiled or toasted on the cob, or the grains can be cut from the cob and pulped, to be made into soft, steamed bread. The Shongwes love this season of eating green maize. Children who live away from the homestead come home at weekends to enjoy it. Together they get through as many as sixty ears a day. It is an extravagant way to use the maize. Each ear eaten green means less maize stored for the rest of the year. But the Shongwes are usually lucky with their crop and have become accustomed to this extravagance. To the Nestors,

fresh from the supermarkets of London, where food has no seasons but is flown in from every quarter of the globe all year round, having fresh maize was no treat at all. 'I'm not getting used to eating maize. I don't think I'll ever get used to it. There's the smell of it everywhere, on your clothes, in your hair. Even the wet washing stinks of maize.'

At the beginning of March one of the fields of maize that had been planted early was ready for harvesting. By now the dried-out maize plants stood six feet tall, brown and brittle in a field knee-high in green weeds. They had to be hacked down, one at a time, with a heavy blade. Then the ripe ears had to be snapped off their stalks and stripped of their crisp, enfolding leaves. It was hard work. *Babe* Shongwe had gone back to work, Lynn had gone to help in the hospital and Robert was busy trying to set up his hot-dog stall in Matsapha. *Make* Shongwe, Mandla and Thandi laMabuza toiled in the field and then carried the heavy crop to the kitchen. They had not yet constructed a new maize-storage rack, and the old one was too rickety to risk. The white ears were piled high beside the wood stove like white teeth. *Make* Shongwe went through them, lovingly picking off mouldy grains to feed the chickens. Mould had spoiled much of their crop the season

Rural life revolves around maize. Here the early green ears are being stripped for boiling.

before and she was taking no chances. She expected to have all their maize harvested by the end of April, and out on the rack to dry once the last rains had fallen.

The cooler, dryer winter months, May to September, are more relaxed. The one major remaining task is to shell, as the Swazis say, the dried maize, usually in August. The grains have to be removed from the cobs. This can be done laboriously by hand, or the task can be shortened by putting the ears into sacks and thumping them repeatedly with a heavy club, to loosen them. You can also rent a shelling machine. The owner of the machine usually asks to be paid in kind: one hundred-pound bag for every fifteen filled. The homestead provides the labour, filling the sheller

with dried ears and bagging the grain. In the old days, grain was stored in giant woven baskets or in clay-lined pits beneath the floor of the cattle *kraal*. Nowadays most people use a corrugated-zinc grain tank with a padlocked mouth, which they buy from enterprising metal workers up and down the country. This protects the crop against rats and mice, but not against insect infestation, for which a noxious chemical tablet is prescribed, the fumes of which kill everything – including, from time to time, unfortunate children.

There are several grain tanks on the Shongwe homestead. Each household has one, in which the woman stores the crop from her own fields. *Make* Shongwe's tank takes up half of her small verandah. This season's harvest looked good. She expected to fill her tank when the crop was dry enough to store. The previous year had been very disappointing. 'We got a lot of maize, but it got spoilt because it kept on raining. The maize rotted in the fields.' Within weeks of the Nestors' arrival her tank was empty. They were already buying from their neighbours. This was unusual, for they generally grow enough to last from one season to the next. But since *babe* Shongwe has a good job in town, they could afford to buy some, as was expected of them, for with their eight children they are heavy maize consumers. Were they penniless, they would be given grain from other homestead tanks. Instead they receive a share of cooked food from the other homestead kitchens.

The harder the maize grains, the better they keep, but the further they are from being

A watchful eye. As homestead head, umkhulu *is responsible for everything, from the allocation of fields to keeping the peace.*

The hand-grinding of small quantities of dried maize is children's work.

easily eaten. There is still more preparation before maize becomes food. Most grain is ground into fine meal, from which the main Swazi dishes are prepared. This is hard work for the daughters-in-law, no matter which method is used. The old way was to grind the grain between two stones: one large and concave, the other rough and round. This is still a method that the Shongwes use for certain dishes. Thandi laMabuza taught Lynn how to do this with soft green maize, kneeling on the ground and letting the weight of her body do the work. All grain offered to the ancestors must be prepared in this way; not only will the ancestors appreciate the trouble you have gone to, but, being by nature conservative, they will be pleased by the perpetuation of tradition. Food for very young babies must also be prepared in this way; only stone-grinding can give the meal the finest texture necessary for a newborn's digestion.

Nearly every homestead has a hand-turned maize grinder, bolted to a stout pole. They were exported to Swaziland from England at the beginning of the twentieth century, as English demand for such things dried up. The cast-iron wheels have survived the century: in pretty lettering, 'Maldon', 'Essex', 'England' are embossed on every wheel. Swazi children learn to read the raised letters, tracing them with their fingers. 'England' is a familiar word in every home. The hand-grinder crushes the maize coarsely.

Much more commonly used than either of these methods, however, is the power-driven mill. All over the country enterprising men with capital have established mills, using either the national electricity supply or a petrol-driven generator. There, for less than forty pence in 2001, people could have a twenty-five-pound bag of grain transformed in minutes into maize meal.

Most maize is carried by women to the commercial mill two miles away.

The difficulty is getting the maize to and from the mill. If you live close enough, you send your son with a wheelbarrow, or your daughter or daughter-in-law carries it on her load-bearing head. The Shongwes rely on their daughters and daughters-in-law to carry the maize to the mill. Thandi LaMabuza does the four-mile round trip every week on foot. People who live too far may have to hire a truck. Because of the transport problem, some entrepreneurs have now invested in mobile mills, which they set up temporarily in more remote areas for days at a time, until local demand has been met.

A lot of energy goes into the milling of maize. Distributing it is equally demanding. *Umkhulu* and *babe* Shongwe need their share to be brought up to Mbabane, where they live during the week. So does *gogo* laBhembe, *umkhulu*'s last wife, who stays near her workplace in Mbabane. Needy relatives arrive and are given a share, and leave weighed down, often with a child to help them. Children are despatched on long bus journeys, lugging heavy loads of maize to and from bus termini for their fathers and mothers. Men seldom carry loads of this kind. In the Swazi division of labour, as in so much of the rest of Africa, women and girls, using their heads, are recognized as the skilled carriers.

Besides maize, the Shongwes grow the other traditional Swazi storage crops: pumpkins, beans, groundnuts and jugo beans. Robert was invited to help plough the bean field on his first day on the homestead. First, the plough oxen had to be fetched down from their mountain grazing. Ploughing is the oxen's most important work. The herd has to be managed to ensure that there are always at least six healthy mature, trained oxen available for this work. Young oxen have to be broken to the yoke. The oxen first dragged the plough down to the bean field, mounted on a traditional wooden sledge. Then the ploughing began, with one man to lead, another to hold the plough and a third to walk beside the team cracking the whip to keep the oxen in line. The whip is about twenty feet long and made of hide. In the hands of an expert it cracks like rifle fire. Daniel found this quite easy. Robert found it impossible. Even with experienced oxen in the lead, a team of six oxen is unwieldy. Robert tried holding the plough down as they lurched up the field, with Themba shouting to him to keep it down and keep it straight. He might have made a good ploughman, but there was no time to develop any expertise. It was his first, and last, ploughing of the season. When the Shongwes went a few weeks later to plough

Cattle herders learn their skills while still young, by caring for the homestead goats.

again and plant their beans, Robert was away looking for work.

Lynn helped to plant the beans. Chloe and Callum went too, but the oxen scared them and they sat under a tree and watched. Three men worked the oxen and plough. *Make* Shongwe and Lynn followed the plough, dropping beans into the new furrow. Two people followed them with hoes, covering the seeds. Lynn enjoyed herself; what she enjoyed most was improving on the traditional method of planting a row at a time. She planted two, and even three, rows at once. She wanted to be the first to finish. When *make* Shongwe told her that she was 'number one', Lynn got quite carried away. She described the traditional method as 'the sheep syndrome' saying, 'I did that for a good hour before it occurred to me that I didn't have to do it the same way as everybody else. So the next time I walked down the middle and did two furrows at a time. *Make* Shongwe said, "Oh, that's very clever!" But it's not. It's common sense.' Lynn attributed the Swazis' lack of innovation to the fact that they were beaten as children. 'No lateral thinking,' she went on, 'or you might be hit.' She was saving time – she did not explain why, or for what purpose.

Besides these storage crops, the Shongwes also grow more exotic and perishable vegetables on their irrigated fields. Surpluses of the perishable crops are sold. *Gogo* laKhanyile, assisted by *umkhulu*, has such a garden on one side of the homestead. On the other side *babe* Shongwe, assisted by Mandla, grows cabbage, lettuce, spinach, tomatoes and onions from seedlings that he buys in Manzini. They cost less than two pounds for a hundred seedlings, 'but their roots get tangled and some die'. He also grows carrots, marrows, peppers, chillies, beetroot, potatoes and other local subtropical root crops from seed. In February, when the Nestors were there, the Shongwes were busy digging over the vegetable plot for the winter growing season. The area is too small for ox-ploughing. A team of oxen is like six bulls in a china shop. They would trample the small beds of carrots and spinach into the ground and veer into the maize.

The Shongwes also keep dozens of domestic fowl and a few geese. The geese graze in a tight white flock on the grass verges of the homestead. They waddle, and hiss threateningly at outsiders. Their gobbling at night kept Lynn awake. 'The noise pollution here has to be heard to be believed. Dogs, roosters, cows, goats, geese! And I thought London was noisy.' The fowl come in every size and colour. A few unfortunate ones are kept in coops: these are the exotic broilers, which *make* Shongwe sees as the start of a commercial enterprise. Factory farming is rare in Swaziland, but the government is encouraging close confinement and forced growth of exotic breeds of poultry as a source of cash. At Zombodze school the children are given four-week-old exotic chicks to rear as part of the agriculture curriculum. At the end of term they get to own the fattened broiler, and have some appreciation of what it has cost them. *Make* Shongwe plans to construct a substantial fowl house very soon, and to fatten broilers there.

The free-range native fowl strut and scratch noisily about the homestead all day long, as they have always done, clucking and cackling, scuttling in and out of people's kitchens and houses, getting under their feet, pecking at every scrap. They brood in pretty grass nesting baskets thrust into trees, and on top of sheds and fences, out of the way of hungry dogs and mongooses, which might

otherwise take the eggs. 'If you find a dog which takes eggs, you take an egg and boil it till it is very, very hot. Then you give it to the dog and hold his nose while he cries and cries. He won't take eggs again.' When the eggs start hatching, the chicks have to be lifted down to the hen. Callum and Chloe loved the chicks and wanted to pick them up and pet them.

The Nestors, as Lynn observed, were too sentimental about animals to make good farmers. The Shongwes keep the poultry for their meat rather than eggs, and also for cash. They slaughter them with economy – not more than one a week. Neighbours sometimes buy them, live, for the equivalent of about one pound fifty. 'We can't eat our own chickens all the time. They'll all soon be finished.' Robert, Daniel and Chloe, keen meat eaters when they first arrived at the homestead, initially shied away from the moment of slaughter. Robert thought the children would have nightmares after seeing the creatures being killed. 'We bypass all this sort of thing in England. I prefer it that way. I don't like to see animals suffer.' Lynn's attitude was more pragmatic. She thought it educational and felt that they ought to know where the meat at the supermarkets came from.

The flock of geese are being bred to sell rather than eat; their free-range diet is supplemented with spoiled grain.

Encouraged by make *Shongwe, Chloe came to enjoy gutting and plucking fowls.*

The people of the homestead kill chickens routinely. They hold them down by the wings and use a sharp knife to cut the throat. Sometimes they pin the dying bird to the ground with their feet until it has jerked its last. The Nestor children became fascinated by this gruesome business. Despite much urging, Lynn refused to try her hand at slaughter on the grounds of her incompetence – 'It wouldn't be fair on the chicken' – but when a goat was killed, to feed the guests at a funeral, she stood by Callum, who insisted on watching. It was an unfortunately protracted business. It took two men all their energy to hold the animal still as, its throat slit and bleeding, it bravely refused to die, kicking over the bowl in which its blood was being collected. Lynn could not stomach it. 'It's barbaric! It's horrible! It's taking too long!' She went inside. Callum howled to be allowed to stay and watch, and did.

There was another source of meat whose killing Callum enjoyed: locusts. *Make* Shongwe casually pulled off the legs of the fat locusts that she came across as she harvested the maize, and popped their dismembered bodies into her apron pocket, saying, 'Nice. This is meat. Children like it. Fry them till their feathers are roasted. It's a delicious meal. That's why it's important to have pockets at harvest.' Callum brought the mutilated, half-alive creatures to his parents and was delighted when Lynn squealed in distaste at their missing legs.

Encouraged by *make* Shongwe, Chloe came to enjoy gutting and plucking fowls. She liked the smell of the warm, wet feathers. She was intrigued by the orderly, colourful arrangement of the fowls' insides, the way everything came out in one hot handful: the tightly packed heart, liver and lungs; the trailing intestines. When she grows up she wants to be a vet.

Thandi laMabuza efficiently kills a chicken for the pot.

CHAPTER SEVEN
daniel goes to school

On his sixth day in Africa, Daniel started school. In Swaziland schooling is neither free nor universal. It is a privilege, for which people are prepared to work hard and make sacrifices. And they do. However, although nearly all Swazi children start school, only half of them complete the first seven grades of primary school. Some drop out through academic failure, others through the inability of their families to afford the cost. Costs vary from school to school. Besides fees, which are modest, and school funds, which are set by each headmaster, the family must pay for books and uniforms. By lowering or raising the school-fund contribution and by requiring children to wear simple or elaborate uniforms, schools can determine whether they attract the poor or the rich. The really rich go to the few expensive private schools.

School fees are due at the start of each year, and rise with each grade. So while nearly everybody can afford the first few years of school, education becomes more and more of a burden for the family, the further you get. By the time you are fifteen or sixteen your family will seriously consider whether your time could not be better spent elsewhere – earning money, if you are lucky; helping relatives who will pay for your keep; or simply helping at home. At the start of the twenty-first century, of the half of all children who went on from primary to secondary school, only a quarter completed form five, the highest grade offered.

(opposite)
Daniel, at just thirteen, was probably the tallest boy at Zombodze National Primary.

The Shongwes take schooling seriously. While the Nestors were on the homestead the local community triumphantly opened its own pre-school, where some twenty toddlers and infants immediately enrolled – at about five pounds a month each – to acquire the skills of obedience and English language that would prepare them for 'real' school when they turned six. The pre-school had been built of poles and mud by the community itself. A local teacher was engaged, her salary funded by the children's fees. *Babe* Shongwe eagerly enrolled Welile and Mphondi. It seemed a perfect opening for four-year-old Callum, since everybody was new to the school, the medium was English and the building was only a few hundred yards from the homestead. But Callum felt just a bit too new and strange to manage it, and Lynn did not want to push him.

All of the homestead's school-age youngsters were in school. *Babe* Shongwe had five children of his own there, and was at the same time paying fees for his brother Dokta's children and worrying about the schooling of the children of his other brother, Mandla. *Umkhulu* still had seven children of his own in school, and two still too young for school. Even those who fail a grade are sent back to try again. Mark, aged nineteen, was repeating form four and so was Mfikile, who at twenty-two was too old for a government school (twenty-one being the limit). He was attending one of the many 'academies' that have sprung up to exploit this determination to acquire valued qualifications.

Qualifications are what education in Swaziland is chiefly about. School teachers, as those who set and mark the examinations that pupils annually sit in the competitive struggle to gain qualifications, are the guardians of this resource. They are the repositories of information that the children will need to receive if they are to succeed, and are duly respected. The classroom is the serious focus of this exchange. Children are required to be passive,

Come rain or shine, school assembly always takes place in the open air.

receptive and obedient. The teacher's word is law. The teacher always knows best. Children who do not do exactly what their teacher says are 'not serious', and must be punished. They are wasting their family's precious resources. Teachers are expected by families to discipline children who frivolously waste their time in the classroom.

Everybody works to maintain this order. Punishments are physical, public and, for the most part, consensual. There is very little emotion attached to either their administration or their reception. Intense emotion is discouraged and anger frowned upon. When agreed rules are violated, agreed punishments are administered. In this way the rules are being reinforced and the social fabric is preserved. Physical punishment is routinely administered in Swazi schools. The parents like it; the law allows it. Daniel knew about this from his first day at school.

Zombodze National Primary is an illustrious school, not because of its academic record (which is perfectly average), but because it is the oldest government school in the country, and because the late and famous King Sobhuza the Second went there, the first Swazi king to receive formal schooling. A plaque on the grubby wall of the earliest classroom commemorates this, and attributes the building of the school (by the British colonial authorities in 1908) to insistent pressure from his grandmother, Queen Labotsibeni, who ruled Swaziland for more than thirty years.

Zombodze was then a royal capital, and the early pupils were all children of princes and councillors. But since each Swazi monarch must establish his or her own new capital, all that now remains of the once-royal village is a dense collection of run-down houses around a neglected Great Hut whose reed screens – once the object of devoted annual tribute labour by the country's virgins – lurch in ragged disarray. Here live the descendants of descendants of princes, people without title but with proud memories. Their children still

School uniforms are compulsory at all Swazi government schools. The bare-footed are sometimes sent home.

go to Zombodze school. Once a year the king sends the school an ox to slaughter, to commemorate the royal connection.

The girls wear plum-coloured cotton dresses and shoes, if they can afford them. The boys wear khaki shorts and white shirts. The teachers are educated, a cut above the rest, sometimes married to men of substance, proud of their position and aware of their responsibilities. Some are driven to school in well-upholstered, well-sprung four-wheel-drive vehicles. Others live behind the school in the modest government houses that go with the job.

When the school bell rings in the morning, the children, who have been playing noisily in the school grounds, sometimes for hours, assemble between two rows of classrooms and start to sing hymns of their choice in sweet, spontaneous harmonies until a teacher strides along the raised concrete platform and greets them in English. English is the rule in all schools. Pupils who speak to each other in their own tongue are punished. By means of this fierce regime children slowly acquire their second language, the one that will open the doors to better-paid work, the one through which they will have to impress their examiners. Some teachers find it almost as difficult as the children. Even at the university frustrated teachers break into siSwati when they need to get a fine point across.

After a prayer and a hymn the children swarm to their classrooms for the earnest business of the day: learning. Lessons follow one another at a dizzying pace: esoteric facts about marsupials, black holes, Peruvian civilizations, perfect numbers, imperfect fractions, longitude, the French revolution, square roots, the passive voice. After two days Daniel observed, 'They teach you much more than in English schools.' The teachers are also more demand-ing. There is only one right way to do anything – the teacher's way. No space here for creative solutions to problems. Pupils who do anything differently are hit; they are hit for any infringement. When Daniel's teacher introduced himself to the class on the first day of term, he showed them the stick with which he intended to beat them when they were 'not serious' about their work. He described the stick as special medicine to help the children: unpleasant but effective. He waved the stick before the class. 'Do you see how big the stick is? I simply go for the buttocks, to help the children pass, to help the students behave themselves… I like to run for the buttocks. I run for the' – he paused and waited for the children to chorus 'Buttocks!', which they did with evident enjoyment. This collective repetition of the teachers' last words is a favourite local teaching device. It stops children from falling asleep. Where teaching is in the second language, as it is in Swaziland, it also serves to improve pronunciation and extend vocabulary.

The Nestors learnt about the local corporal punishment regime from Daniel on his second day at school, when he came home and told them cheerfully, 'I got back late from lunch and almost got beat.' He had lingered at a new friend's house during the lunch break and the teacher was annoyed. 'She said we'd get beat next time. I think I would of got beat today, but it was my first time. She said next time she'd beat me with her medicine stick.' Lynn and Robert were appalled and determined to prevent Daniel from experiencing physical punishment, even if it meant taking him out of school.

All their frustrations of the previous week with African ways of doing things were suddenly released into an issue on which they were sure of the moral high ground. Hitting children was wrong, particularly in school. All of Europe agreed with them on that. Threatening to hit a new boy for a minor breach of rules was unacceptable. Lynn said, 'In England we spent years abolishing child labour, corporal punishment, child abuse.'

Robert remarked, 'I don't hit any of my children. I'm not going to send him to school for other people to beat him and discipline him. If anyone's gonna beat him, it's gonna be me.' There was nothing pacifist about Robert's response. Deep-seated resentment against authority surfaced. He was all for an instant confrontation. 'I'll have to go and tell 'em straight, "You put your hand on that child and I'm gonna come and sort you out." I don't care who they are. They could be the head-mistress or whatever. "Don't hit my child!"'

Lynn recognized that by sending Daniel to school they'd entered a contract, but by keeping him there they were compromising their own principles. 'They've got a rule: chil-dren who do wrong get beaten. If we go to school we abide by the school rules. He gets beaten. But if he gets beaten, and beaten severely, we take him out of school. One beat-ing will be enough.' A day later she saw *make* Shongwe hit her two adolescent daughters with a stick for failing to wash out the cooking pot after the evening meal. It confirmed her view. 'Now I've seen it. Daniel isn't going to get beaten or he comes out of school.' They urged Daniel to 'keep his head down for the next nine weeks', but if the worst came to the worst, he should run for it. Lynn instructed him, 'Avoid a beating whatever way you can.' Robert said, 'I've told him, if they try to beat him, to come home as fast as he can.'

The cane is a normal part of every Swazi teacher's equipment.

Daniel, innocent of his parents' moral outrage, was confident that he could avoid punishment. 'I probably won't get any beats if I'm good.' But in this he was wrong. Within a week he was part of a group of ten called in for two routine strokes each for poorly executed work. He followed his parents' advice; he watched the others line up, but when it came to his turn he walked off. The teacher was unperturbed. The disciplining of one temporary foreign pupil is not worth getting steamed up about.

The Nestors decided that they would have to ask the school for an assurance that Daniel could be made an exception. The school accepted Daniel's exceptionalism with equa-nimity for the weeks he was there. They were less pleased when, after a few weeks, the Nestors failed to notify them of their decision to take Daniel out of school. Only a week beforehand Robert had said, 'He's a thirteen-year-old boy. I want to keep him out of trou-

ble. I don't want him messing about on the homestead. Let the teachers educate him. At home he'll just get under his mum's feet.' Now all his resolve crumbled. Daniel reported children being beaten 'black and blue… every day'. Lynn, with some exaggeration, thought that Daniel was 'in mortal fear of his life'. In Robert's opinion, the school's academic results were achieved through 'violence and child abuse'. He commented, 'They need to review the whole situation and find a better way to educate children.' He decided to avoid confrontation. 'It's not down to me to start a revolution here, 'cos I won't be here to finish it.' Daniel would finish school that very week. 'That's it. I don't want him coming home every day saying he nearly got hit by somebody. School is something you're meant to enjoy.'

Lynn observed, 'When we came here there were obviously going to be things we could not come to terms with, and this is just one of them, one of the things we're not going to accept.'

Corporal punishment was not the only reason for this decision. Contrary to Robert's prediction, Lynn had never got into the school-run routine. The journey to and from school remained a major obstacle to be surmounted each day. Although they were finding the walk easier than on that first day, it did not get any shorter. Lynn resented the early start if Daniel was to walk to school with the other children. Rising at five to get to school was 'not reasonable in any society'. She did not see how children could go

Once the novelty had worn off, Daniel found school very boring.

all that way on foot and still do a full day's work. The weather was another problem. It was usually very hot, but sometimes it rained. 'If it rains I can't see myself sending him. *Make* Shongwe sends hers, whatever the weather, but I can't see myself doing it. Anyway, Daniel will refuse, point blank.' They were incensed that the unreliable bus gave priority to long-distance adults, often forcing the children to walk the full six miles each way.

Lynn had never been committed to sending Daniel to school. Sitting on the pavement in Manzini before term even started, deploring the length of the queues of parents waiting outside the banks to pay their children's school fees, she said to Daniel, 'I actually don't give a toss whether you go to school tomorrow or not. It'll be a damned sight easier if you don't, to be quite honest.' She felt she was quite capable of teaching him at home, and that he would be back in what she thought of as a 'real school' within ten weeks. She had no intention of queuing. She said smugly, 'I don't do the queue thing.' She found queuing ludicrous, crazy. She thought it slightly contemptible that people should so passively accept the arrangement. 'There are enough people at the bank queues to cause a complete riot, but they're happy just to chill out for eight hours.' She never did queue to pay the school fees. She left the money for Daniel's overdue fees with *make* Shongwe the day before they left the homestead.

Daniel himself saw the teaching and the curriculum as the main problem. Although at the start he had enjoyed the novelty of learning to slash down long grass and weeds with a piece of flat iron ('It's quite easy when you get into the swing of it. We should do agriculture in school in England.'), he came to resent the hours each day that he and the

other pupils were required to spend in manual labour: washing the classroom floor, cleaning windows, sweeping the playground, cutting the grass. It was part of the Swazi culture of child labour that the Nestors found so unenlightened. As for the schoolwork, he was bored. He thought he knew more than his teachers. He said cockily, 'I could teach the science lesson and the English lesson. I have to correct the teacher's grammar and pronunciation.' Leaving, in his view, had nothing to do with the beatings. 'I'm not bothered about the beatings. I'm a good boy.' He couched his argument in economic terms. 'We're paying for it, so I should be learning something, but I'm not.' He also feared he was missing out on more exciting experiences that the rest of his family were having on the homestead and on frequent, furtive visits to town.

The school, like the country, had disappointed him with its ordinariness. He said, 'They have lots of our customs. They use our equipment. There's nothing really that is actually black.' He had expected school to be 'one room, a hut, sitting under a tree like it used to be'.

When, after a few weeks, Daniel left school without notice, the teachers felt that they had been treated discourteously, used and tossed aside without so much as a thank you. Lynn was lonely and wanted him at home with her. She said, 'He's been to school, he's made friends, he has learnt to cut grass there and to clean the school. He's done all sorts of things he wouldn't have done at home, but now he wants to spend the rest of his time in the homestead, doing homestead stuff, which I think is brilliant. If he doesn't go back to school that's fine, because he's learning all the time. He's getting a much broader education.'

*Every Friday afternoon
the children have to clean
the school.*

Once more the Nestors were stepping out of line with the rest of the homestead. Theirs were the only children to be kept at home. The children's schoolwork frequently took priority over other things. Having rejected the local options of school and pre-school, the Nestors found themselves burdened with providing Chloe and Callum, and now Daniel, with some academic stimulation every day. They called it 'home school' – the kind of thing colonials in far-flung places, spurning both native facilities and boarding schools, had invented in the mid-twentieth century to keep their children abreast with the syllabuses back home. It was a practice completely alien to the Shongwes, who saw teachers as specially qualified specialists, whose place they would not presume to supplant. The Nestors had no such inhibitions. It was another of the decisions that set them apart, the implications of which, for their homestead participation, passed them by. Unlike the other adults on the homestead, they were seldom available in the mornings to share in any of the work of the homestead. Instead they were inside their room, on their bed, encouraging Daniel to write in his diary, teaching Callum the alphabet and Chloe spelling and tables.

From this time on, Daniel missed out on the daily sociability of the long, leisurely walk to school that the rest of the children of the

neighbourhood shared and took for granted. He missed out on the collective homework sessions, sprawled on *make* Shongwe's verandah, arguing over the correct answers with Xolile and Cebsile, and trying to keep the dust, chickens and babies off their exercise books. Now an exception, Daniel saw less of the homestead's children because he spent less time with them. He was quite interested in cooking, but as a boy he was not entirely accepted into the kitchen by the women of the homestead. He made fires and boiled water for Lynn, but she did not think it right that he, as a child, should wash the family laundry or scrub the floor of their room.

It was hard to keep Daniel interested in home school. Despite Lynn's earlier assertions of her competence to teach him, they had not come prepared. There were no books and she confessed herself short on patience. So he tagged along behind Mandla and *babe* Shongwe and the herdsman, as any boy dropping out of school would. He climbed the mountain to look for cattle, did a bit of gardening and helped to repair their thatched roof. He had a go at milking the homestead's four cows in calf and accompanied the cattle to the dip. The tasks were intermittent; conversation was limited by his inability to talk siSwati. He got bored. He wanted to go home.

Despite the cane, school is a happy place for most Swazi children.

CHAPTER EIGHT
livestock and lineage

On his very first morning in Swaziland Robert had climbed up the mountain to bring the Shongwe cattle down from their communal grazing to the homestead. It was a heady experience, but he was too taken with the excitement of the scenery to think about the cattle. By far the greatest proportion of every chiefdom is set aside as communal grazing land, for the Swazis are enthusiastic cattle keepers. Cattle occupy a critical position in their society. They are the form in which people keep their wealth. Whereas in the West, farmers regard cattle as a means to wealth – land, houses, money-in-the-bank – in Swaziland cattle *are* the ultimate possession, wealth itself. Nobody sells cattle unless they are in a very tight corner. To sell cattle is to lose wealth. Swazi behaviour in this respect is by no means irrational. Conservatively there will be a 10 per cent increase in the herd size each year through calves. In 1982 an expert reckoned that the return on cattle in Swaziland is 27 per cent per annum, far more than could ever be earnt on savings in a bank. But it is a risky form of saving. When in 2001 an outbreak of foot-and-mouth disease prompted the government to slaughter several hundred cattle, compensation was offered at just seventy pounds a head – about half their market value.

But to think of cattle in terms of the market is to misunderstand their value to Swazis. When they say that a man without cattle is nothing, they do not mean simply that he is poor. They

(opposite)
The importance of cattle in the symbolic, domestic, social, economic and spiritual life of the Swazis cannot be overestimated.

The Shongwe cattle have to be brought down to the kraal *once a week in order to be ready for obligatory dipping against ticks the next morning.*

mean that he is unable to be part of the complex system of cattle exchange and debt – an essential part of the social system. Everybody seems to owe somebody cattle, and to be owed cattle. This arises very simply from the fact that every time a man impregnates a woman for the first time, he thereby owes her family cattle. Since Swazis have hitherto scorned contraception and prided themselves on their potency and fertility, and since (at almost six births per woman) they have one of the highest birth rates in the world, there is a great deal of cattle debt binding people together. These debts are increased by the institution of polygamy. In Swaziland, polygamous by tradition, it is always legitimate for a man to seek new sexual conquests, even if he is already married. If he should not just impregnate but marry such a woman, he would owe her family yet more cattle.

The Shongwe homestead was, and had been, embroiled in several such transactions. Thandi laMabuza'a husband, Amos, *umkhulu*'s firstborn, was bought from his mother when he was four. *Umkhulu* said, 'We Shongwes decided to take Amos with us. We bought Amos with one of the cows paid for damages to his mother.' The practice whereby Swazi fathers 'buy' their children from their girlfriends' kin is an old one. When a man impregnates a single woman, he immediately becomes liable to pay damages to her parents for spoiling her, and thus reducing her value on the marriage market. He can, and often does, right this wrong by agreeing to marry her. In this case the damages he pays are discounted from the *lobolo* due to her parents. At the time of the Nestors' stay, *Umkhulu* was waiting to receive cattle from four men who had impregnated three of his daughters.

Men always have the right to the children they have fathered, provided that they pay for them. The price is set by custom at two cows for a girl, one for a boy. Mandla Shongwe was preparing to buy his three children from their mother, a woman he once hoped to marry and for whom he had just completed a house at Ekudzeni. He was still bitterly nursing his wounds. 'She decided to fall in love with another man while I was away working in the mines. I tried several times to talk with her about this. Even my brothers tried to help, by talking with her. She told them she had no business with me.' *Babe* Shongwe said, 'The children are two boys and a girl, from one of his girlfriends. They do not live here. They sometimes come to stay. We are going to buy them. When we get money we shall buy cattle to send to their mother's family. How much cattle will depend on how many we can afford and how many we think they deserve. We are still going to meet as a family and decide on that. Usually it's compulsory that you pay the five cows for impregnating their child. As for us, we are going to decide whether we pay three cows or the five required.'

The parents of single girls used to insist on keeping such children until the proper payment had been made. However, the changing economy has put a considerable strain on this practice. Children are no longer considered the unmitigated economic blessing they once were. Rather than contribute to the homestead economy through their labour as fetchers and carriers, nursemaids and herders, they have become a cost, requiring school fees, school uniforms, textbooks, shoes, bus fares and, from time to time, fancy food like tinned pilchards and corn crisps that only money can buy. Many parents of single mothers are pleased to have the toddlers taken away by their fathers' kin, without the payment of any cattle. 'Let their father feed them!' Thandi laMabuza said that Amos was loath to buy his children for just this reason; they would be too expensive to maintain.

Although such exchanges are always fiercely negotiated, the number of cattle that are due is fairly standard: about fifteen head to marry a firstborn daughter, and twelve for subsequent daughters; up to five head for being the first to impregnate a girl, and two or three for subsequent pregnancies of a girl already 'spoiled'. Ideally, a girl's family receives cows driven on the hoof from the man's family *kraal* to that of her father.

This was how *umkhulu* married *gogo* laKhanyile in 1970. They had met two years before when she had just left school, having completed the primary grades. She was ready for marriage. As she says, 'I fell in love with my husband.' Their first child was born a year later and Elizabeth called him Sipho, meaning 'gift', 'because I regarded the child as a gift from God.' It is still common for marriages in Swaziland to begin with impregnation and birth. In this way the all-important fertility of a woman is proved before a man's family commits itself to the marriage. The king himself serves as a model. The women he chooses as official lovers, *maphovela*, remain mere girlfriends, concubines, fiancées (the search for an appropriate English word is impossible), distinguished as such by their unmarried dress, until they give birth.

By 1970 young *umkhulu* Shongwe had amassed the requisite twelve cattle to marry, and Elizabeth officially joined the Shongwe homestead as his new wife. Sitting in the Shongwe yard thirty years later, she recalls the occasion with pride. 'We arrived in this place for the wedding on a Friday. The dancing was on Saturday and it went on until Sunday. They *teka*'d me the same day of the wedding in the presence of my parents. On Monday the Shongwes sent me back home. That is the custom. There my father prepared the traditional brew for those who were coming to bring my marriage cattle, *lobolo*. Then I came back to the Shongwes to collect the people selected to take the *lobolo* to my family. That was when they paid twelve cows, including the one for my mother, to wipe away her tears, *insulanyembeti*, and one to be slaughtered for the feasting at my home, *lugege*. This was a big occasion and I liked it, because at that time I was a young girl and everything was great. It was a good day, one never to forget.'

Although the *lobolo* is set at so many cows, in practice the girl's family often agrees to a compromise; some (but never all) of the cows can be paid as money. Just how much money each cow represents is once again negotiated, but is always less than the market price. This device allows every woman to say, proudly, that her *lobolo* was fixed at ten or twelve cows. It saves face. The *lobolo* cattle are rarely delivered in one transaction, if for no other reason than

that pregnancy has usually already occurred: the first 'instalment' has normally been paid early as compensation for 'damages'.

Umkhulu's last wife, *gogo* laBhembe, joined the homestead at Ekudzeni eighteen years ago, when she had already borne the Shongwes two children and was pregnant with a third, but her family did not receive the bulk of her *lobolo* until 1996, when she was pregnant with her seventh child. They received seven cows. 'Three were real cows, the rest was money. He paid it to my grandfather.' Within three years all that remained of this *lobolo* was one cow. One had been killed by a snake, and another had been slaughtered at the wedding feast of a kinswoman; the money had been put into her mother's bank account, but the bank book had been stolen when her mother died. In 2001 two cows were still owed to her kin: the two special beasts whose exchange signifies the conclusion of the marriage transaction. *Umkhulu* hoped to pay these later in the year, at the traditional wedding dance, but *gogo* laBhembe had qualms about this. She had recently converted to an American sect that discouraged such a ceremony. She wanted to be married in church instead. 'I have already informed my husband about that. He does not support the idea, but at least he knows about it.'

Babe Shongwe tried to explain some of this to Robert when they went up the mountain again, about a month later, to bring the cattle down to be dipped. Robert asked

(opposite)
In February four of the Shongwe cows had calved and were giving the homestead small quantities of milk. Milking, like all other activities associated with cattle, is the work of men.

where the cattle came from. 'Some are bought, some are from the *lobolo* system. When someone is married he must pay *lobolo*, like ten cattle, to the family.'

'Is it like if my daughter got married, I'd have to pay for her wedding?' asked Robert.

'Yes,' said *babe* Shongwe misleadingly, misunderstanding the question. In fact it is not remotely like paying for your daughter's wedding. It is not even like paying for your son's wedding, though this comes a little closer to it.

Robert saw the cattle as an economic asset, and made simplified assumptions about how the size of the herd must determine the Shongwes' economic standing and hence their social circle. He supposed that a man with only

five cattle would not be 'on the same level' as the Shongwes, with a herd of more than forty, and that therefore they would not let their daughter marry such a man. Not at all, said *babe*. Indeed, princes apart, Swazi society is characterized by a marked egalitarianism. He now tried to explain the system to Robert. His explanation was brief but difficult and took too much for granted. He said, in effect, that if his daughter had a child by such a man, he would demand those five cattle and use them to complete the *lobolo* that he still owed the parents of his own wife. He put it more cryptically. 'There is a system that is being used by the Swazis. The firstborn can carry *lobolo* for her mother.'

৪০ ଔ

The Ekudzeni grazing lands are awkwardly located on the top of the mountain. There, unrestricted on a high grassy plateau, the Shongwes' forty cattle graze with those of their neighbours and of the king. The king is the country's biggest cattle owner, but only a few of his cattle graze on the Mdzimba mountains. By custom they are distributed over many different chiefdoms. The chief in each instance appoints a local man as their keeper. The royal herd, which is never required to work, like the herds of commoners, is wild and frisky, stampeding as the herders try to separate their own from among the several hundred cattle on the mountain.

'How do you know which are yours?' Robert asked, perplexed. 'Are they marked?'

Daniel waits with the Shongwes' cattle as one by one the homestead herds are called to queue for dipping.

'They are not marked,' *babe* Shongwe replied. 'You can see by its colours that this is yours.' He also knows to whom the other cattle belong. 'These cattle belong to my cousin, a certain Dlamini homestead. This ox belongs to King Mswati the Third.' Swazis know their cattle intimately, and each addition is an event. The history of the family can be told in its cattle.

Six of the Shongwes' cattle are the remains of the *lobolo* paid to them in 1999 when *gogo* laBhembe's first daughter married. She was, as her mother proudly reported, as yet the only one of *umkhulu*'s nine daughters

Each animal is goaded to take its turn to jump into the poisonous water. They swim frantically, noses in the air. Sometimes they drown.

to have brought cattle to the homestead. Her *lobolo* was 'ten cattle, real cattle. In fact there were eight, but two of them were pregnant so the calves were also counted.' But one pregnant cow was stolen and 'slaughtered by thieves' who, when apprehended, compensated them with a calf. Two were slaughtered during the wedding feast itself. Another was paid to 'a person who would help recover a four-year-old child [the granddaughter of *umkhulu*'s deceased sister], who disappeared from the homestead one day while driving cattle from the *kraal* with her big father.'

It took two and a half hours for Robert, Mandla and *babe* Shongwe to get to the top of the mountain. They passed a woman gathering grass and a man with a gun hunting wild animals. 'Wild animals!' Robert was excited. 'Like what?' Wild pig, baboons, monkeys and jackals, *babe* Shongwe told him casually. He shouted to the hunter to confirm this. His voice carried a long way. This is a technique that the Swazis have developed to save their energy. Protracted conversations can take place between people a mile apart.

Babe Shongwe told Robert that this was the route he used to take when walking to Mbabane as a boy, before the roads were built. *Umkhulu* still sometimes went this way. From the top of the mountain the country spread out in every direction. *Babe* Shongwe pointed out chiefdoms and homesteads. The landscape was intensely familiar to him. He had been coming up here since his mother first came to live in the homestead, when he was about twelve.

It took more than an hour to find and round up their cattle. While Robert ran about helpfully like a sheepdog, panting, to head them off, Mandla and *babe* Shongwe shouted instructions and pointed out which cattle were theirs. 'Not that one! The red one, yes, that's it! Leave the black one.' They whistled piercingly, mournfully, to encourage the animals, and cracked their whips, shouting 'Hiya! Hiya!' They followed the cattle down the mountain. 'They know the way.' The descent was slow because, they said, they did not want the cattle to 'lose meat'.

The cattle dip the next day was like a fair. There were hundreds of lowing cattle and dozens of men: some old, the owners of the homestead herd; others young herdsmen. *Babe* Shongwe introduced Robert to two of his fathers. They asked him about his cattle in England. He said that he had none. Ah, they said, he had goats then? Robert, the Londoner, replied, 'No. We've got parks, but we use them for recreation. There's not enough space in London.' They commiserated with him. They said life without goats must be very expensive. 'If we want some meat, we slaughter a goat. It is very dear to buy meat from butcheries.'

The air was loud with the cries of calves and the throatier bellowing of frightened bulls and oxen. All the cattle from the chiefdom were there, to be counted and registered by the dip-tank officer, who sat shouting out people's registration numbers and making entries in a large official book. Dipping against disease-carrying ticks is compulsory.

Owners are fined one pound for every absent animal. Each animal was goaded to take its turn to jump into the poisonous water: bright khaki and thick with the dung of terrified animals. They swam frantically down the tank, their noses in the air, whites of their eyes shining. *Babe* Shongwe watched one of his calves anxiously. Sometimes they drown.

It is difficult to overestimate the importance of cattle to the Swazis' sense of well-being. The most apparently urban of Swazi men is likely to have cattle somewhere. You have only to scratch a diplomat, a civil servant, a university lecturer to discover a cattle owner. He needs only to ensure that somebody is herding them, watching over their health and taking them to be dipped against disease-bearing ticks some thirty times a year, in dipping tanks provided by the state. This is easily arranged. He can put them into the protective custody of a relative or friend. This practice is known as *sisa*. It is much favoured by the very rich, whose abundance of cattle can be an embarrassment. It is a bit like a rich friend in England lending you one of his cars for a year. People enjoy having the care of a big herd of cattle, even if they belong to somebody else. They site the cattle *kraal* in the middle of their homestead, the better to enjoy them. They value their dung as fertilizer, building material and, when necessary, fuel. They enjoy their milk, which they share judiciously with the calves. Sometimes a person looking after another's cattle under the *sisa* system has the right to a calf a year, and can use the practice to establish his own herd. *Sisa* is not the only option. Unemployed adolescents who have fallen out of the educational system can be hired as herders for pocket money and their keep. The Shongwes paid their herdboy, a distant relation, about fifteen pounds a month.

CHAPTER NINE
praising god and the ancestors

On their fourth Sunday in Swaziland, the Nestors, having shared the Shongwes' prayers to God and the ancestors in the Great Hut, accompanied some of the family to church. Most Swazis are deeply religious. They see their lives as powerfully controlled by spiritual forces. There are the spirits of their deceased ancestors, whom they will one day join, and the newer spirits introduced by Christian missionaries. Missionary rejection of the benign power of dead ancestors accounts in part for the growth and strength in southern Africa of the hundreds – if not thousands – of independent churches, where ordinary people feel spiritually safest.

In the theology of these independent churches God is almighty, *Nkulunkulu*, creator of heaven and earth, unknowable, inscrutable. He is god of the universe. The ancestors, by contrast, are the homestead's own private spirits of dead kin, knowable because remembered, but transformed, supernatural and able to intervene in the affairs of the living, for good or ill. After some initial resistance in the nineteenth century, the Swazis took to Christianity with a fervour that is still unabated. They enjoy the Bible. The Hebrew history of wars, defeats, invasions, kings, tribes, flocks, tribute, polygamy and levirate (the practice of marrying the widow of one's brother) speaks to their own experience. They have little difficulty in incorporating the Christian Holy Spirit into their cosmology: spirit possession, both benevolent and malevolent, is a

(opposite)
Between customers, a stall-owner reads the Bible.

common African experience. *Umkhulu* said, 'There is no difference in my opinion between the Holy Spirit and the ancestors. It can happen, when you are sick, that the Holy Spirit heals you. It can also happen that you consult the ancestors and are healed. I do not condemn either. The two are equal. They both come from God.'

By the middle of the twentieth century more than half of the Swazi population claimed to be Christian. That proportion has certainly increased since then. Most of the Shongwes see the relationship between the Christian God and the ancestors as a very simple one. They pray to both. The ancestors have the slight edge in day-to-day affairs, because they are more knowable. People say when they pray that they have in mind their grandmother. One of the first things that happens to every newborn Swazi baby is an official introduction to the spirits of their paternal ancestors. It is this belief that simplifies the question of paternity among the Swazi; no woman would jeopardize her child's fortune by misleading her family about who its father was.

Ancestors must be thanked for the homestead's good fortune, and propitiated in the event of misfortune. The day-to-day fate of the homestead and its members is interpreted as the outcome of ancestral will. When something good happens to a person – a lift from a stranger, a gift, promotion at work – they are likely to exclaim, 'The ancestors are with me today!' When something bad happens – failure in an exam, the death of livestock, an abortion, crop failure – they are likely to wonder why the ancestors are displeased, and may sacrifice a goat and brew a special ritual beer to restore their ancestors' favour.

There is never anything impromptu about communication with the ancestors. They are approached ritually, with due preparation, through the oldest man in the family, who signals to them with the spilling of specially brewed beer and blood, usually of a goat, though a chicken will suffice. In rich homesteads and on highly significant occasions, an ox is killed. Even the ritual sacrifice of people is not unknown, but is hedged in secrecy, only occasionally spilling into the press as 'medicine murder', about which there is considerable ambivalence.

When the Shongwes knew that a British family was coming to stay with them, the first thing they did was inform the ancestors. They brewed the beer and killed a goat, which was pulled, bleating and resisting, from the cattle *kraal* to the Great Hut. While one of the sons of the homestead held it upright by the front legs, another plunged a knife expertly several times into its heart, until it collapsed, lifeless, on to the ground. As it fell, *umkhulu*, standing barefoot between the Great Hut and the *kraal*, called upon God and the ancestors to look with favour on the coming of the British family. The goat was then disembowelled, skinned and hung beside the beer in the Great Hut.

When, next morning, the stiff carcass was brought out for butchering, the goat's skull was fixed above the doorway of the Great Hut and a small strip of goatskin was bound about the wrist of *make* Shongwe, to serve as an aide-memoire to the whole community that the ancestors had been consulted. All the related families from the neighbourhood came on that occasion, as they always must, to eat the meat and drink the beer. *Make* Shongwe, a teetotaller where Western alcohol is concerned, happily affirmed the intoxicating nature of the brew. 'It's what we like when we go traditional. We get drunk, even the women, but not so much. The women just take a sip and go. The men finish up.' The celebrations included gathering in the Great Hut for prayers, followed by dancing, singing and clapping. The ancestors enjoy a party.

Ancestors are considered particularly important in matters of health and illness. There are many specialists, expert in communicating with the spirit world, practising as healers in Swaziland. For those fortunate to display the necessary skills, this offers an easy way to earn a good living. There are two main types of healer, the *sangoma* and the *inyanga*. The distinction between the two, once sharp, is now blurred. The *sangoma,* or diviner, is usually a woman. Her calling is precipitated by a mysterious illness – the sort that would unhesitatingly be described as a mental breakdown in the West – which is taken as a sign that the spirits have chosen her. To resist might be fatal. Training takes the form of apprenticeship to an established practitioner. The *sangoma* works through spirit possession. The *inyanga,* or herbalist (the 'medicine man' of nineteenth-century Western travel romances), is usually male and works through interpreting thrown bones. However, there is now no rigid division between the techniques of these two specialists: when Robert and Dokta consulted a *sangoma* about their unemployment, she used both.

As a British nurse, Lynn was asked by the Shongwes one day to accompany an elderly father of Themba's to the hospital; he had deteriorated during treatment from a *sangoma* and his brother thought the time had come for Western medical intervention. Lynn was very accepting of the traditional healing techniques; she supposed it was like alternative medicine in Britain. She said, 'The *sangoma* wants him to return when the hospital has revitalized him. It's good the *sangoma*

The Great Hut, indlunkhulu, *where all important homestead matters are discussed, is dedicated to the ancestors.*

wanted him to come to hospital and get some X-rays. It means the patient has an informed choice. It's his body, his life. The *sangoma* is alternative therapy. I'm sure he's very knowledgeable.' She thought the doctor's diagnosis might help the *sangoma* to prescribe the proper herbal medicine.

This attitude was rather sanguine. Traditional Swazi healers operate within a framework of assumptions of cause and effect that is very different from both Western medicine and the popular newer alternative therapies. Diseases are believed to arise either through ancestral anger or through witchcraft, and treatments are directed at appeasing the ancestors or identifying and counteracting their bewitchment. People may be bewitched by swallowing magical substances, by walking over them or simply by being close to them, typically buried in the ground, but sometimes transferred during sexual inter-

course. Such substances are believed to cause swellings, pain, paralysis and even death. On the other hand, some traditional therapies (like enemas, inhalations and vomiting) are more akin to Western practice. Most Swazis are willing to try both medical systems, and categorize their afflictions into those that are better treated traditionally and those that are better taken to the local clinic. The clinic is usually the cheaper, but not necessarily the most effective, option.

℘ ℭ

In most of the independent African Christian churches that flourish in southern Africa, people escape the cultural domination of Europe. In small local congregations people's religious imaginations are allowed free rein. Churches are among the most vigorous local institutions. Church dues, frequently a full one-tenth of hard-earned cash, feature

Filled with the Holy Spirit, exuberant Christians dance their way home for an all-night vigil.

prominently in people's monthly budgets, along with hire-purchase furniture instalments, burial-society payments and other onerous responsibilities.

Most churches have their own distinctive uniform. The further a church is from mainstream Western Christian denominations, the more important and elaborate its uniform is likely to be. Roman Catholics, Anglicans and Methodists expect only a distinctive blouse for women. The independent churches expect the men too to wear special church clothing. Long white, green and blue coats – often decorated with appliqué crosses, arrows, moons and stars, and worn with broad embroidered sashes – have become the sign of Christians, who throng the roads on Sundays going to and from the intense three-hour Sunday morning services or all-night vigils. The men are often dancing in an excess of joyous spirit possession.

Of all the independent churches in Swaziland, the wildest is undoubtedly the Jericho Church, founded in the 1970s by the charismatic Merika Vilakati from Mankayane, whose unusual powers were heralded at his equally unusual birth. 'When he was delivered a dove preceded him from his mother's womb, and he was born with all his teeth.' He was brought up in the puritanical, white-robed Zion Christian Church, the ZCC, the biggest of the independent churches in the region, but in the 1970s, while in South Africa, he 'got the power' and broke away to establish his own church. His followers were nicknamed the 'red gowns', his being the first independent church to choose bright red for their men's uniform. Trimmed with bright-green fringes and topped with a bright-blue cape, the Jericho uniform attracted immediate attention, but the church grew through its ability to attract more than this. It also attracted young uneducated men in great numbers, who enjoyed its vigorous rituals, its face-to-face wrestling with the evil spirits, its uninhibited possession by the Holy Spirit and its relegation of the Bible (and the literacy this entailed) to the very fringe of worship. *Umkhulu* explained, 'They find that when they stop to read the Bible they lose the Holy Spirit.'

The *emajeliko*, as they are called, rapidly established a reputation for unusual spiritual powers, especially healing. It is alleged that they get this power from the confluence of rivers: 'They go to big rivers, where two rivers meet and the water keeps turning. They sink down on that point. There are certain powers that they get at that point. Anybody who wants that power can try it. Many of them disappear and are never seen again.' People flocked to Vilakati's headquarters and readily paid for healing of all kinds. He became a very rich man; cows, children, five or six wives.' Following biblical prohibitions for Jews, the *emajeliko* abhor pork. They have a reputation for being able to detect it on people's breath days after it has been eaten. Suspected pork eaters are sometimes severely beaten during Jericho church services.

They are also very proficient at detecting witchcraft. 'When somebody has bewitched you, maybe burying something to kill you, their spirit can tell you that there's something buried there. They can pull it out, if you call them. You don't have to pay them, you just give them an offering, maybe twenty *emalangeni*, maybe a hundred, not a payment.' Like most independent churches, the Jericho Church embraces ancestral spirits in its pantheon, where they have a lowly place, not unlike that of patron saints in the Catholic spiritual hierarchy.

The Jericho church at Maphondweni is the nearest church to the Shongwe homestead. It is for this reason that some of the Shongwes attend its services. The nearest Zion church, to which most of the homestead belong, is several miles further along a mountain track. *Umkhulu* says, 'I attend that [Jericho] church since my church is far away. I think they also belong to God, like other churches. I do not think there is anything mysterious or sinister about it.' You reach Maphondweni from Ekudzeni by crossing the river and climbing up a steep hillside. The church, which lies just over the brow of the hill, is built of mud walls under a rusting roof of flattened oil drums, which overlap each other like giant tiles. On the sagging wooden door a large white cross has been painted. The small windows have wooden shutters, not glass. From the church you look past the pastor's substantial house down into a quiet green valley crisscrossed with red footpaths. Goats graze on the slopes. Far below, the brown river winds lazily. When the congregation pauses in its praises, you can hear it burbling.

Inside, the light shines through the nail holes in the roof like stars, illuminating four crowns of thorns that are suspended, one over each of the four quarters of the room. On the grey walls large yellow-ochre lettering proclaims WE LOVE JESUS and JESUS IS THE ONLY ANSWER. There is one candle above the simple mud altar. In the centre of the church a large pole supports the roof. An enamelled basin of water is suspended by string from the roof beam; not holy water, but something to damp down the dust when the service gets under way.

Like many such churches, it has slipped into semi-independence; this is the secret of its vigour. Individuals of inventive imagination are rarely constrained by tradition.

Intensely local, churches respond to local needs and ideas. The Maphondweni *emajelikos* no longer wear red; they can, and do, devise their own church vestments from whatever materials they can afford. Some are in riotous colours to match their religious fervour: plum-pink trimmed in green and yellow; green trimmed in black, gold and red. One, a poor man, wore sackcloth trimmed in blue. All wear capes about their shoulders and the distinctive Jericho headband around their foreheads, in rope, twisted wool or braided ribbon. Women wrap their heads in close-fitting colourful caps.

It was here that the Shongwes took the Nestors one Sunday. Lynn and Robert dressed sombrely and carried their Bible. Daniel defied Swazi convention and, like a girl, carried *make* Shongwe's youngest child strapped to his back. They waded through the river and up the hill. The service, as always, began gradually; people without watches who walk long distances cannot time their arrival, as Western churchgoers do. Early-comers pick armfuls of sweet-smelling grass to sit on around the edge of the dung floor. Then they wait – men to the preacher's left, women to his right – singing simple repetitive hymns in complex harmonies, until the congregation has swelled sufficiently for the main ritual to begin. Daniel and Robert sat with the men; Lynn, Chloe and Callum with the women.

The congregation, probably inspired by the visitors as well as the Spirit, gave of their best. The choir of adolescent girls sang sweetly but inconsequentially, 'Jericho, that is the place for me. I want to sing a song about Jericho.' The congregation swayed and prayed and sang. They echoed the pastor's amens and hallelujahs. They formed a joyful dancing queue to shake each of the Nestors

Members of the Jericho church devise their own vestments from whatever materials they can afford.

While the pastor beats time with his stick, the men run rhythmically round and round the centre pole, breathing in unison like the bellows of an old church organ.

(opposite)
Possessed by the spirit, an entranced zealot climbs high into a tree outside the church, rips off the branches and carries them round and round the church.

by the hand to welcome them. Then, in their distinctive Jericho ritual, to the rhythmic chanting of the women sitting around the edge of the room, the men (accompanied by a few bold women), with sticks held aloft like Swazi warriors, began to trot around the centre pole to the rhythmic pounding of sticks on the hard earth floor.

At first they ran slowly. Then, at a signal from the preacher, the pace quickened, the women retired one by one and the men closed in around the pole, running faster in close formation, a choreography of bare feet in perfect step. As they ran, they started to breathe in unison, making a harsh sound like the wheezing bellows of an old church organ. The women standing round the edge continued to sway and sing their plaintive harmonies, led by the preacher who periodically broke into rousing prayer and preaching. After a full twenty minutes, the men came to a sudden halt and, turning to face one another, slowly sank to their knees, still breathing like bellows. One by one, they were seized by the Spirit and, talking in tongues, spun off into private ecstasies inside the church, bouncing on the walls, shaking their fists and shouting incomprehensibly at the windows.

Outside the church the Spirit seized them more vigorously. Veins distended, jaws tense, in hoarse pairs, they spoke in tongues. They seemed to be engaged in some ritual competition as each responded to, and modified, what the other had shouted. Their speech was peppered with Portuguese, Zulu, Afrikaans and English words, some of them obscene. They spat. They foamed at the mouth. They did somersaults. They climbed trees. They lifted huge rocks and ran down the hill with them. They tore branches off trees. They leapt high into the air. They fell on each other and rolled on the ground. They knelt beside each other and howled into each other's faces. They thumped one another and tore at each other's clothes. Their frenzy lasted a full hour. All the while the preacher, inside, preached while the women listened and prayed and sang. Little children, dressed in their Sunday best, came and went, stepping unconcernedly past the tumbling, noisy men, carefully taking off their shoes at the church door. Then suddenly all was calm. The possession was over. One by one the men shyly got to their feet, dusting down their clothes.

The Nestors watched and listened. At first Lynn was spellbound. Caught up in the infectious enthusiasm, she said halfway through the service, 'It's how a church should be. They give so much to God on a Sunday, it's mind-blowing, so much joy and energy. This is working for the Spirit, definitely. This is hard work, putting every ounce of their being into praising God.' She found the intensity of it all uplifting. 'On top of a mountain in the middle of nowhere, praising God. This is it. I'm very glad that I came, to see the commitment.' Somewhat surprisingly, it made her

In pairs, possessed men talk to one another hoarsely in tongues.

feel closer to home. 'It renews you, gives you a sense of purpose, strength to face next week.'

Daniel thought it was 'much more interesting than church at home'. He was nursing a large lump on his forehead, accidentally acquired as he had mimicked the zealots banging their heads on rocks. He said he might join in the running next time. He might talk in tongues. Chloe thought it was 'scary'. Callum sat on his mother's knee, eating an apple, and said nothing at all.

Robert's reaction was very different. He had sat impassively through the service. He rarely goes to church in London, but that was the standard by which he judged the *emajeliko*. Back on the homestead he dismissed it as 'primitive'. 'I didn't relate to it at all. I didn't hear much mention of Jesus Christ, and all the rest of it. One of them looked like he was trying to have sex. The rest looked like they were on LSD, tripping.' The athlete in him viewed their heavy breathing with disdain. 'They worked themselves up and got knackered. Just huffing and puffing.' He went on, ' Some people might get into it. Not me. I wouldn't go again. I wouldn't take my kids there again, neither.'

Robert validated his rejection on many grounds. The service was two hours too long. There was too little emphasis on the Bible, and people didn't even take Bibles with them, though all Swazi children have to have them for school. 'Three verses from the Bible in three hours is not the way. You'd have thought they'd have studied the Bible. They didn't use it the way I know the

Bible should be used.' There was no moral instruction. 'All those children were not being taught things, like how to share. I never heard any of that. Just some geezer rolling on the floor and another one slapping him on his back.' He doubted that the spirit possessions were real. Their behaviour seemed 'contrived'. People were too careful about bumping into one another. 'If you're in the Holy Spirit you don't mind who's in your way.' But more than that, he wondered what spirit it was that was possessing people. 'It didn't look like there was any religion there at all.' He asked with a cynical laugh, 'What's the Holy Spirit doing bouncing people off walls?'

Robert's strong views reshaped Lynn's. The talking in tongues did not bother her at all. She had met charismatic Anglicans at home. 'Stuff like this goes on at home, but inside four walls.' But she worried about the finer theological points. She explained to Daniel that there ought to have been others there inspired to interpret what the Spirit was saying to those who were possessed. She conceded, 'There was a slightly mixed message going on there. There did come a point where we lost the Holy Spirit and ended up in mass hysteria.' She concluded, 'It's too charismatic for us. I don't think I'd go back.'

Robert had the last word. 'If that's the way they worship, good luck to them, but it's not the way I do it, and I don't know anybody else who does it that way, either. I've sampled it, I've looked at it and I don't like it, and that's the end of it. I've tried it out. I didn't say I'm not going up there 'cos there's just a bunch of idiots running round a pole.'

It was at this point, after two and a half weeks in Africa, riled by the Jericho church service, that Robert made his position in relation to African culture clearer. There was noth-

ing patronizing in his approach. 'I've come here to see what it's like. I haven't come here to write things off without trying them out. I'm giving everything a chance. It's down to me what I take and what I don't. That's the way they run this country: they take things from us, from Europe, they take what they like; and the bits they don't like, they leave behind. I'm doing the same thing the way I'm living here.'

Some Swazi Christians, following missionary precepts, have rejected the ancestral cult and joined orthodox denominations or embraced one or other of the American-style charismatic ministries that spring up every year, promising miracles and delivering electronic organs, microphones, loudspeakers and choirs, as seen on television. Those who have television sets, and those who aspire to them, are attracted to their glamorous services. *Gogo* laBhembe and Mark have joined such a church, and so has *make* Shongwe's son Senzo. He took the Nestors there a month later, one Sunday in February.

The church, an unpretentious barn set in the middle of a maize field, was packed with men in suits and ladies in fancy hats. The preacher preached fire and brimstone and the congregation shouted 'Hallelujah' and 'Amen'. Lynn, herself a keen participating Christian in London, was familiar with some of the songs and sang along. Afterwards she said to the pastor, 'You should come and preach in our church in London some time.' Robert, who is 'not 100 per cent into religion', sat aloof and impassive, sceptical of the central place given to the ritual of the offering, the collection plate, and of the way people abruptly shook off their spirit possessions as the electric organ stopped playing to mark the end of the service. As he says, he prefers boxing.

CHAPTER TEN
keeping order

Corporal punishment in schools is simply an extension of the way children are punished at home. Swazis think children should be disciplined with physical, rather than emotional, force. The emotional blackmail to which the West is at present so widely, and often so smugly, committed, works only in emotionally intense, small families. In the looser, extended families of much of the rest of the world, the threat of some adult's disapproval weighs less heavily on children. There are always other people about, just as important to you, who can take their place in your affections. Punishment is more effectively delivered as a sharp slap, the swift thwack of a stick on the legs, or a more deliberate lash across the hand or buttocks for grosser misdemeanours. The right – or, as Swazis would say, the obligation – to administer such punishment rests with all adults, just as the responsibility for caring for children does.

Child-rearing is a collective task, not the narrow responsibility of the biological parents. The fact that every Swazi child has several people whom he or she can call 'mother' and 'father' implies this. *Umkhulu*'s son Mark recited all the people whom he called 'mother': the three wives of *umkhulu*'s brother, *umkhulu*'s four wives (including, of course, *gogo* laBhembe, who bore him) and all the sisters of these women. Their younger sisters are his 'small mothers', their older sisters are his 'big mothers'. He says 'father' to all the husbands of these women, as well as to *umkhulu*.

(opposite)
Umkhulu, at breakfast in the men's enclosure, resents the intrusive camera. As homestead head he expects deference from all.

Umkhulu's youngest child, Phetsilie, kneels at her mother's door, awaiting permission to enter.

The husbands of mothers' sisters are likewise ranked 'my big father' and 'my small father', according to their wives' birth order. The terms 'father' and 'mother' mean something very different to Swazi and British offspring. When Robert went to the cattle dip he was perplexed when Themba introduced two strange men to him as 'my father'. As far as Robert knew, Themba's real father was dead, and *umkhulu* was the substitute. He had not yet grasped just how many fathers Themba had. Lynn was just as confused when she was told that the sick old man she had been asked to accompany to hospital was Themba's father.

As Swazi children learn to talk, they absorb a diffuse relationship with 'mothers' and 'fathers', rather than the intensely focused relationship with 'my mother' and 'my father' that is so central to the Western family. The matter goes deeper than mere labels. In principle, the lifetime obligation of offspring is to *all* these parents. In practice, some relations will be perceived as closer and will come first, but there is always a second tier of fathers and mothers, sons and daughters, should the need for such kinsmen arise on either side. This obligation is reinforced in their day-to-day experience of growing up in a formally structured group, where position is more important than personality.

As Lynn began to grasp this web of kinship, she said, 'Everybody is either a brother or a father!' But she was wrong. Not all your relatives of your parents' generation are fathers or mothers. Your mother's brothers are your uncles, *umalume*, a distinct category of kin, not to be confused with your father's brothers, who are your 'fathers'. In a traditionally ordered homestead like the Shongwes', you grow up with your father's brothers; you share their name and their ancestors. Your mother's brothers belong to quite a different set of kin, bearing a different name and protected by different ancestors. As closely related outsiders, they are highly valued as indulgent kin, whose sympathy you can rely on. Your *umalume* is your ally.

Equally distinctive are your father's sisters, your aunts, or *anti*, not in any way to be confused with your mother's sisters, who are your 'mothers'. Your father's sister is also known as your 'father', but this time the Swazi word has the feminine ending – she is your 'female father', *babekati*. If your father and all his brothers were to die, *babekati* can take his place in the family hierarchy, as your 'father'. It is for this reason that women, as sisters, often hold more authority in their brothers' homesteads than they do, as wives, in their own. They are still remembered by their brothers'

Lynn and Chloe. This British nuclear-family behaviour, emotive, demonstrative, stands in stark contrast to the formality of Swazi kin relations.

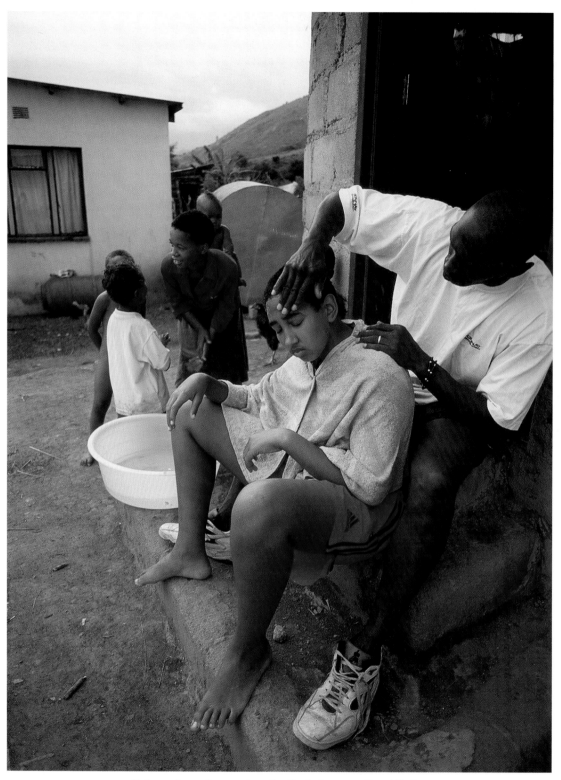

Robert, the caring nuclear-family father, cuts Daniel's hair.

ancestors, who protected them before they left for marriage. On all important occasions they must be at his Great Hut to share in the deliberations.

The contrast with the emotionally close – sometimes suffocating – Western nuclear family could not be sharper. Swazi parents frequently live apart from each other. One hundred years of labour migration have accustomed the Swazi wives to absent husbands, but to imagine that labour migration is responsible for the quality of the bond between parents is to misunderstand the African family structure. A glance at the nuclear family helps us to appreciate what the African family is not. The nuclear family of the West is completely couple-centred. It begins with the joining of two people who have chosen to live exclusively with each other. They are expected to live on their own and set up their own house. The Western wedding, with its wedding presents, is about establishing this new house. This couple forms the heart of the nuclear family, which exists only as long as they choose to be together. Their delight in one another's company and their sexual attraction to each other are considered essential prerequisites for the marriage. Their disillusion with one another is sufficient cause for the marriage to be dissolved. When one or other leaves the family is said to be broken.

This couple usually has children. They alone are responsible for looking after these children, supervised by the state, which sets the rules: so many weeks in school each year, for so many years; so much space for each child to live in; and so on. Once children are mature they cease to be the parents' responsibility. Exactly when this occurs depends on different circumstances and places. The children are expected to leave home, and not return. They are expected to find their own partners and, in due course, to set up their own independent families on the same pattern. Every time people marry they create a new family. The ageing parents are still regarded as a family until one or other dies. This marks the end of their family. The last remaining parent may go and live with one of their children's families or may live in an institution specially designed to care for the elderly, during the last years of their life.

The African family is based on descent rather than marriage. In Swaziland families are based on paternal descent; you get your family name and identity from your father, who got it from his father, who in turn got it from his father. (Your mother likewise got her family name from her father, but this does not matter very much to you, because her family is never your family: descent is paternal.) You are likely, as a child (whether you are a boy or a girl) to live with both your father and your father's father, because all the males in the family stay put. Of course you also live with your mother, and all the other wives of all these men, and all their children. If you are a boy, you never leave this family. When you grow up, you bring your wife to this family, as your mother was brought in by your father, and as your grandmother was brought in by your grandfather.

If you are a girl, your experience is quite different. You have to leave the family you were born in and go and live with the family of your husband. You do not lose the name of your birth family, but you cannot confer it on your children. Your children belong to your husband's family, not yours. Even if you are unmarried, your children's birthright is to belong to their fathers. Married women are for years outsiders in their husbands' home-steads. Getting married for a woman means the formidable business of joining her husband's strange, established family. When *make* Shongwe was asked, in December, if she was looking forward to the Nestors' arrival, she said, 'It is like getting married. You stay with somebody you don't know, yet you have to stay with that somebody.' A married woman has to be introduced to her husband's ancestors, who have to be asked to extend their protection to her. By the end of her life she will have become so familiar with his ancestors that she joins them.

In practice, all sorts of things happen to upset these two patterns, but the patterns are nevertheless there at the backs of people's minds, influencing the way they act and judge each other. The Nestors have a nuclear family. Lynn has never known anything else,

although Robert's childhood family experience as the child of Caribbean immigrants was somewhat different. After his father left his mother, he shared a household with his mother and her sister. Textbooks describe the families of most ex-slave societies as matrifocal (mother-centred), rather than couple-centred. Robert refers to his childhood family as an extended family, because the important members included living-in aunts.

Lynn insists that she too has an 'extended family of friends' in London, but this is a caring voluntary network of friends – as reliable only as their feelings towards one another, as stable only as a nuclear family marriage. Her network runs on emotions. The Swazi kin network runs on rules. Sex, age and birth-order shape the position that you and others occupy, and the expectations that people consequently have of you. The Nestors

No distance between the generations in this kind of family.
Chloe and Callum help Robert take a bath in the river.

never grasped this system. They treated *gogo* laKhanyile with an unseemly lack of respect by Swazi standards, waving to her and shouting, 'Hello, Cocoa!' They were being friendly and egalitarian; they had no understanding that they were being rude.

The homestead is an integral part of the system of law and order on which the rest of society has been constructed. Homestead heads hold authority by virtue of their office, not by virtue of their gifts of leadership or persuasion. *Make* Shongwe takes notice of what *umkhulu* thinks, not because he is clever or wise or because she is frightened of him. (Nobody could be frightened of him, for he is a mild, gentle man with a perpetual smile.) But he is *umnumzane*, head of the homestead. He speaks with authority conferred on him by the chief. His authority comes with the weight of the whole Ekudzeni community behind it. Who becomes homestead head is a matter of heredity, but each new head must be confirmed by the chief every time an old head dies. *Babe* Shongwe might have seemed the most important person on the homestead to the Nestors, because he was young, sure of himself and fairly well-off, but these are not criteria that the Swazis use. *Umkhulu*'s was the final word, and everybody knew it, even if, in that other world of cash and employment, he was just a gardener.

The amount of land that he controls is also affirmed by the chief. Most land is inherited, but inheritance is not automatic. Whenever a man dies, the chief in council considers the inheritance in relation to the heir's needs and competence. Has the new heir sufficient family labour to work his father's fields? Has he a wife at home to help him? Are his children strong enough to work the land in question? Are the boys nearing marriageable age, and about to bring in useful wives to swell the labour force? Another way of acquiring a share in this land is by swearing loyalty, *kukhonta*, to some particular chief. In this case the chief will expect you to have done your homework, to have identified a piece of apparently unoccupied land on which you wish to settle. The elders then consult widely with potential neighbours, to make sure that the land really is unallocated and that other community members have no objections to your membership. Lynn said, 'Robert has been asking about how to get a piece of land. Apparently you only have to give the chief a cow.' It is not so simple. Strangers cannot be admitted without the king's permission. Even for Swazis, *kukhonta* can sometimes take years.

※ ※

The Great Hut is not only an ancestral shrine but a family court room, and *umkhulu* is the judge. He sits with a lot of assessors; everybody in the family is invited to have their say, and they do. The Nestors attended these sessions, but unfortunately, because they generally could not understand what was being said, they missed the flavour of this particular grass-roots participation. The acting chief for Ekudzeni explained how day-to-day problems are approached in rural communities. 'Domestic disputes and squabbles are addressed and settled in the homestead, if possible. If the people of the homestead are not able to reach a settlement, they will call in the elders from their extended family to assist them. This family council has the power to fine wrongdoers a goat or a cow, depending on circumstances. That animal will then be slaughtered and eaten within the homestead, by the elders and other kin. It is

Esangweni, *the men's enclosure, where men discuss affairs informally as they eat and drink.*

not good luck to keep it. If the offender is a woman, she may be sent back to her parents to be reprimanded by them. Her parents must then return with her and negotiate a settlement with her in-laws. If the family elders are unable to reach a settlement, the case is referred to the chief's inner council.'

The Shongwe family were grappling with the problem of Dokta's unproductive household while the Nestors were with them. Dokta and his wife were summoned to the Great Hut to have their financial and marital arrangements scrutinized by everybody. The matter had not yet reached community level; the Shongwes were sorting it out between themselves. There are no private problems among the Swazi – all problems are shared. This is a relief, but also a penance. Lynn described it as like living in a goldfish bowl.

People who are unhappy with the homestead's decisions and judgements can take the matter to the chief. His is another hereditary office, this time one that has to be confirmed by the king. Although chieftaincy is hereditary, the rules concerning who succeeds whom are open to argument, the rightful heir often a matter of dispute. This ambiguity and vagueness are the essence of an intensely local system in which local power is continuously contested and negotiated. The lack of written rules is essential to its performance. This is, of course, anathema to the modernizers, who long for written, published records and regulations, for uniformity and consistency, for a system that will take the power from the oldest men with the longest memories and put it in the hands of young bureaucrats. An American-funded programme to codify Swazi law and custom was re-launched in 2001.

The acting-chief at Ekudzeni hears disputes with the aid of six assessors elected by the people. They form his inner council, *libandla lencane*. Only if the inner council is unable to reach a decision will the matter be referred to the whole community, meeting as the Great Council, *libandla lenkhulu*. Meetings are held in the open air, under a tree. Anybody from the community is entitled to attend and express his or her view. The court reaches its decisions only after all opinions have been heard. Appeal after this is to the king and may take years. The community is called together in this way whenever necessary. Months may pass without such a meeting, especially in the busy growing season, when men's time on their fields is at a premium on their weekends back home.

Umkhulu has been a member of the inner council for the past eight years. This council, like the Great Council, acts as a court on all domestic and minor criminal matters. It also has powers to fine, but this time the livestock are given to the office of the chief himself. This is one of the few rewards for office. Chiefs also receive gifts from people to whom they grant land, but even when this gift is money, the land is never considered bought or sold. Some chiefs receive an annual honorarium from the royal purse. In 2000 this was rumoured to have increased from about £50 to £150 a year. Chiefs are unlikely to be, or appear, any richer than their subjects although a chief can command the labour of

his subjects to work on his official fields, from which he is expected to brew the beer with which to refresh them.

The chief's fields at Ekudzeni and his official seat, *umphakatsi*, were reputed to be in a sorry state during the Nestors' visit. Robert was promised the experience of participating in tribute labour, to weed these fields and clear the undergrowth around the chief's official quarters, but he was never called. The acting chief – a mild, educated man, brother of the late chief – blamed the intransigence and incompetence of his *indvuna*, or chief executive officer. He was looking forward to handing over his powers at the installation of his nephew as chief, but could not be sure when this would happen. It is a matter that rests with the king.

The Ekudzeni community had discussed and approved in December the coming of the Nestors to the Shongwe homestead. One day, shortly after their arrival in the homestead, *babe* Shongwe took Robert to meet the acting chief. Indifferent to the niceties of procedure and hardened against deference, Robert remained standing throughout the meeting and kept his hat on. Afterwards he asked, 'Do you think he liked me?'

Themba replied, 'I forgot to tell you to take your hat off as a sign of respect. You must respect him, because he's the chief of our area. You are coming high and you make the chief confused.'

Robert had mistaken the nature of the meeting – a polite introduction – and had proceeded to harangue authority about what he perceived as the shortcomings at the homestead: no electricity or telephones. It was a cultural misunderstanding. Afterwards he laughed at himself. 'I'm good at putting my foot in it. Next time I'll be quiet and wait to be spoken to.'

CHAPTER ELEVEN
sparing the rod

Almost as soon as she arrived in the homestead, Chloe wanted to run away. And little wonder. Her mother was in tears, and she was about to be displaced as the only Nestor daughter by the arrival in their midst of a strange Swazi sister, Xolile, who had been foisted on them. If her mother was upset, Chloe would be too. Anyway, she felt sick. She had been vomiting and she had no appetite. She did not like the food.

It took Chloe several weeks before she began to enjoy being in Africa, unlike Callum, who to everybody's surprise settled in without a tantrum. In the beginning the only good thing was the river. There are actually two rivers at the Shongwe homestead. The little mountain stream that runs past *gogo* laKhanyile's house joins the big river, the Mtilane, at the bottom of the maize fields. There are lots of different swimming places. The water was deliciously cool in those first hot weeks, and Lynn took Chloe and Callum there every day. They spread their colourful fluffy towels on the grassy bank and lazed and sunbathed, and washed their hair with shampoo, and drank orange juice. In the afternoons Daniel and the other children came too.

(opposite)
Callum found washing the dishes more fun in Swaziland than in London.

Chloe and the other girls skipped. Her dad skipped every day, very fast and seriously, with his special skipping rope from London, but she and the other girls skipped together, chanting rhymes, taking turns with a rope made of grass. When the other girls went

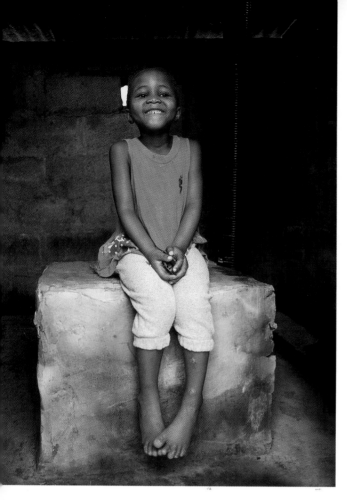

to school, Chloe tried to teach Callum to skip. The girls taught her a Swazi clapping game and she taught them an English one. She also taught them to play noughts and crosses, drawing with sticks in the sand. There was not much else to do. The children did not talk much English and their names were hard to pronounce. They were not like Laurie and her other friends in London.

Slowly she got to know them. They went swimming together. They had competitions to see who could stay underwater the longest, and cheated at it. They jumped off a big rock into the rapids. They chased each other. She found the children kinder than the ones she knew in London. They shared the skipping rope without argument, and the big ones helped the little ones. They were very good at the singing and clapping games and seemed

to enjoy everything more. They never complained when they had to light the fire, or stir the maize porridge or wash the dishes. Xolile came and scrubbed the floor of their house. She was ever so good at it, just like a grown-up. Chloe helped her polish it afterwards – it was fun. She also helped Xolile fill plastic bottles with water for Lynn and carry them back to the house.

It was scary at night – pitch-dark outside, not like London, although they had a night light, a little candle. She was too scared to go to the pit latrine by herself. You could never see where you were going. So she woke Daniel up and made him go with her, because Daniel was never scared. The pit latrine was funny – like a well – and you sat on the wall. No flush. But it didn't smell bad, because they had a pipe to take the smells up into the air above. In the daytime it was full of bees and wasps, and you had to watch out that your bottom didn't get stung. Her mother sprayed it with Doom.

Sometimes Chloe helped Lynn do the washing down at the tap. Their clothes were getting stained red from the earth and it was very difficult to wash off. In London the soles of her socks got black, not red. She missed the black dirt. She missed having a hot bath. She wanted to sit in her room and play with her toys with Laurie. She wanted to go home.

At home school, Lynn encouraged Chloe to compare her life in Swaziland with her life in London and to write about it. In their fourth week Lynn said, 'Chloe has not been overly impressed by anything she's done here so far, but writing about it helps her to see the good bits better.' But Chloe was becoming more familiar with the other children. She could pronounce Xolile and Cebsile. She was picking up a few siSwati words and phrases. She could say 'I'll hit you' and 'Jesus loves you'. She could almost carry things balanced on her head. She was also picking up some Swazi attitudes. So were Daniel and Callum. Lynn remarked, 'The main thing is that they are all getting on better and looking after each other. They used to drive me bananas at home, always sniping at each other, arguing and fighting. Over here they pull together a lot more.' The influences were mutual; *make* Shongwe was less pleased with the effect that the Nestors were having on her children. 'They are copying their ways,' she said sadly.

By their ninth week, when it was nearly time to leave, Callum and Chloe were quite at home with the Shongwes. Lynn described them as 'really happy' and added, 'And if they're happy, I'm happy.' They were free to roam about the homestead in perfect safety. There were no dubious strangers to worry

about, there was no traffic. They had learnt to chase away snakes by making a loud noise as they stamped their way through waist-high weeds down to the river. They had stopped being afraid of the dark. They played for hours on the pile of building sand beside their house, digging tunnels, making roads, building sandcastles. They slid on their bottoms down the steep red sandbank at the back of their house. Daniel tried to make a sand toboggan, but found that empty cardboard cartons were better. They made an aeroplane out of an empty box and took all the children for a ride in it, hobby-horse style. They learnt how hard it was to bowl a hoop made from an old bicycle wheel. They could sing several songs in siSwati, adjusting their pitch perfectly to the mournful cadences of the others.

Chloe had made good friends. She had in fact bestowed the precious title 'my best friend' on Mfundvo, *gogo* laKhanyile's youngest daughter. In Chloe's second last week on the homestead *gogo* laKhanyile taught her how to plait

Dancing games: Chloe, Mphondi, Callum and Welile practise a movement as Robert looks on.

grass and knot it into a floor mat. Mfundvo was just starting to learn this cash-earning craft. Chloe, ever the Western competitor, said, '*Gogo* started to do this when she was twenty. Mfundvo's starting now and she's eleven. I'm only eight.' She loved doing it and declared it her favourite occupation. She sat for hours beside *gogo* in the shade of her house and worked at it while Mfundvo was at school. She said, wistfully, 'I don't think I'll get it finished. It takes two to three weeks and I've only got a week left.'

Chloe declared herself 'really sad' to leave Ekudzeni. She liked the place, the space, the chickens strutting about the yard. She liked doing home school. She liked the ready access to friends without having to go and knock on their doors. She noticed that there were few arguments because there was nothing to argue over. 'At home, because we've got robotic toys and dolls and things, we argue about who's going to have it first. We fight over Gameboys and computer games. They don't seem to fight here, except about who's right in an argument.'

ಬ ಚ

From their first week in the homestead the Nestors had been troubled that the Shongwe children did not play enough. It upset their idea of childhood. It took Lynn only two days on the homestead to sense that her excursions to the river to swim with her children were un-Swazi. She said, 'Perhaps married women aren't meant to be playing in rivers. Women here don't play with children, do they? The children go off and do things.'

To the Shongwes' surprise, Lynn skipped and sang and clapped, like a child, with Chloe and the other children. She spent exhausting hours amusing her children in their room.

Callum's first words upon reaching the homestead were 'I'm bored!' In the Nestors' view, parents had a duty to prevent their children from being bored. The Nestor children are well aware of how seriously their parents take this complaint. Unaccustomed to spending so much time with her children, and deprived of all the usual social and material support, Lynn found distracting and amusing them hard work. But she persevered. She was setting an example. At the end of her stay she said proudly, 'The children here are a lot more like children now. They didn't know how to play till my lot came bowling in and showed them what children in England do – play!'

Robert decided to make a swing the day after *babe* Shongwe left the homestead to go back to work. He said, 'There's nothing for kids to do on the homestead.' It was a substantial British swing, modelled on the kind that you find in London parks: free-standing, enormous and worlds away from the traditional *umjikeni* that Swazi children make for themselves when the urge takes them, using a leather thong suspended from any big tree. Robert's swing was constructed from the tree trunks that the Shongwes had cut down on the mountain and carried home for firewood. He sited it next to *babe* Shongwe's house. *Umkhulu* was not consulted, nor was *gogo* laKhanyile. Robert and Daniel laboured all day, excavating holes for the poles and the supports, wiring poles together, testing the frame for weight and stability. Thandi laMabuza, not much more than a child herself, watched with excitement. Mandla watched in silence. *Make* Shongwe wondered what *gogo* was going to say when she came home and saw 'this town' being constructed in the yard. In her opinion, it was a pity Robert was wasting his time on swings when he could be constructing the maize rack they so badly needed, but she was partly to blame: the treated poles for the rack had not yet been delivered.

The children started fighting over the swing as soon as it was completed. Robert observed, 'That's human nature, isn't it? There's always going to be fights. They'll have to learn how to share. They're getting fun out of it. That's the main thing.' He did not think the swing would last, once he left. 'Playing is not something their kids do. Repairing a swing won't be important to Themba.'

Indeed it was not. The swing was not only divisive, but distracted the children from their work. In Africa – notoriously – children work: not in factories (there's too much competition there) but in their homes. The Nestors knew about this before they reached the homestead. 'You hear that, Daniel and Chloe?' Lynn said playfully when she was reminded about it on her first day in Swaziland. 'In Africa children work. So you'll have to work too!' She had in mind a bit of fetching and carrying. She had no idea that the work children did was serious, sustained; that adults could rest because the children were working.

'Most of the chores – firewood, washing – are done by children,' Robert observed. 'Before they go to school they have to do the washing up. They work very hard.'

In the Swazi view, as in much of the rest of Africa, hard work is an essential part of a child's education. 'The hard way is the best way. They have to learn to know that everything is not easy, that everything is hard.' Of her own children, *make* Shongwe said, 'When they're back from school they take over, they do the cooking. It's time for me to rest. They have to learn to do everything, because when I die they should stand on their own.' She

watched with disapproval as the Nestor children picked and chose their snacks. Deferred gratification is a deliberate part of her programme. 'If she or he wants something, she has to come to me and ask for that. Even if I've got that, I have to be fussy. I have to say, "No, you are going to get this on another day."'

She was, she said, preparing them for a life in which they were going to have to defer to authority: of husbands, if they were wives; of fathers, if they were sons; of employers, if they were lucky enough to find jobs. 'Like now, there's no work to be found. Jobs are scarce.' Thinking of her daughters, she continued, 'The job you can find is only looking after babies and cleaning for somebody else. What if you don't teach your children how to scrub the floor, how to wash, how to cook?' Daniel's agriculture teacher had defended the teaching of practical subsistence skills in much the same way. If, as seemed likely, there were to be no paid jobs for people in the future, they would at least know how to grow their own food on their homesteads.

The effect of this educational philosophy is that children in Africa actually do a lot of the work that needs to be done. Children are looked after by other small children. Girls start looking after babies as soon as they are strong enough to carry them on their backs. Boys and girls run errands. When the neighbourhood pre-school group opened near the Shongwe homestead the week after the Nestors' arrival, the pre-school children took themselves to school each day. *Make* Shongwe's two infants, Welile aged five and Tandzile aged three, each carried three chairs to school on their heads. By the time they are twelve most rural Swazi children can look after themselves and others. Both boys and girls are expected to wash all their own clothes. Girls also do most of the drudgery in the kitchen – lighting fires, filling kettles, cleaning pots, shelling groundnuts, cutting up pumpkins. Boys sweep the yard. They get off more lightly than girls because childcare and the preparation of food on the homestead, which take up so much time, are seen as the preserve of women.

The Shongwes defended their practice with vigour. 'Children,' said *make* Shongwe, 'are the extension of our arms. In Swaziland, it's the children who work. They work more than the adults.' This was perfectly fair. There were more of them, and in time they would graduate to the status of leisured, organizing adults. Work taught the children independence.

This African philosophy of child-rearing is diametrically opposed to the policy of total indulgence espoused by the Nestors. Defending his decision to take Daniel out of school, Robert said, 'Life is hard enough without giving them pressure… Why make it hard for them from day one? Give them a break! It might seem like we're wrapping him up in cotton wool, but that's the way I choose to raise my child. Everyone's got their way of doing things. This is the way I choose to do it. What do you reckon, Daniel?'

Lynn remarked, 'The Shongwes watch me telling Chloe and Callum not to do [domestic chore] things and I think it does annoy them slightly.' She dismissed the notion that her children were spoilt as 'an absolute load of rubbish'. 'Chloe would scrub floors and polish floors; she would do the washing up, she would do the washing, but it's like – a lot of it is my fault, because I don't expect them to do half as much when they're children. That's the way I bring them up. That's the way our society is. She was brought up in England for eight and a half years of

her life. To transport her here and expect her in five weeks to be a Swazi child – it just can't happen. It's a huge amount to ask of an eight-year-old. You can call that spoilt if you like. I just think it's plain and simple common sense.' She found Swazi children's precocious independence 'mad'. 'A kid Callum's size in charge of a herd of cows! I won't let Callum go to the toilet alone. I've seen two- and three-year-olds roasting their own maize on an open fire, pushing it in with their fingers. It gives me a heart attack. Maybe we are over-protective of our kids in England.'

The Shongwes understood and regretted Lynn's position. They viewed the Nestor children's leisured upbringing with disapproval. *Gogo* laKhanyile said, 'I don't like the British way of life. A child should learn to wash his clothes from an early age, so if I die, he can cope.' They all agreed that Daniel was much too old to have his clothes washed by his mother.

'I only wash the clothes of babies, not children,' said *make* Shongwe.

'Their children are very undisciplined. They run around in their socks and are not beaten,' said Thandi laMabuza.

Just as the Nestors thought the Swazi children were enslaved by their parents, so the Shongwes thought the Nestor parents were enslaved by their children. 'These children, they are the type that know their parents will do everything for them. The parents believe the children make the rules,' *gogo* laKhanyile said. 'My granddaughters can't enslave me.'

They marvelled at the presumptuous way Daniel appeared in the kitchen in the morning, expecting breakfast without having helped to prepare it. *Make* Shongwe said, 'I get up, I cook, I dish, and he only comes to get his food!'

Make *Shongwe teaches Welile and Mphondi to carry chairs to their pre-school.*

Peer group pressure. Chloe helps to clean the kitchen for make *Shongwe, who is busy feeding Thandeka.*

Thandi laMabuza remarked, 'I wouldn't do that for a child.'

Gogo laKhanyile said, 'I don't blame the child. I blame the parents. They won't hit them.'

When Xolile was allocated as her household helper, Lynn's first cry had been 'slavery!' and her first impulse was emancipation. Xolile would be released to play, instead. She would show the Shongwes the proper way to treat children. The Shongwes observed and disapproved. *Make* Shongwe said, 'I think it's their way of living in their country. Everything is just freedom in children. In our country it's not like that. Their children like swimming, and staying with their mummy, and taking other children swimming. No washing, no cooking. They do whatever they like. The family is being ruled by kids. They are the ones telling the parents they don't want this, they want this. They are not like ours.'

After Lynn had several times sent Xolile off to swim in the river with Daniel and Chloe, Xolile said that her father had instructed her to wash the floor of the Nestors' (somewhat chaotic) room. Robert said, 'I felt bad about it. I didn't want to jump in and say, "Don't do that!" because her dad told her to do it. I let her get on with it.' Lynn thought it was unreasonable: she was perfectly able to clean her own house. But she saw that she would have to allow Xolile to do some house-work. She decided to watch carefully against exploitation. 'If I can keep it to a minimum. There's ways and means. I can't alter the culture and I can't disrupt it too much, but I can tone it down a bit.'

Lynn's way of 'toning it down' was typically Western. Unable to understand or accept the diffuse give-and-take of the homestead – the sustained indebtedness of each to all – she turned the homestead's gift of labour into a limited transaction between herself and Xolile. She would pay Xolile for her work each time. 'I gave her a dress that's absolutely no use to me. Made me feel better. She'd done a job and earned wages for it.' Lynn did not feel a similar urge to pay the older girls who got up each morning to light the fire that she used to make her family's breakfast, or those who daily searched for firewood up on the mountain.

Lynn decided she would not ask Xolile to do anything she could not ask her own children to do. The effect of this decision was that she found herself asking her own children to do more, which they did with a will. 'It's peer-group pressure,' said Lynn. 'Same as at home. There their friends are playing. Here their friends are working, so there'd be no one to play with anyway if they didn't join in. Last night Daniel polished five pairs of shoes and Chloe polished the floor. Will it last twenty-four hours when we get home?'

It was a rhetorical question, but Chloe had an answer to it. 'At home I don't help Mummy do anything. I don't help her wash, I don't help her polish the floor. I don't help her clean her shoes. I don't know why I help her here.' But she knew why she didn't help her at home. 'At home we've got washing machines. She won't let me wash the floor at home. She says I'm going to trip in the wet bits, and I'll

make the floor dirty. I don't clean her shoes because she doesn't clean her own shoes.'

Robert likewise felt constrained by the homestead's rules about children's work. 'Like this morning: I have to make a fire each day to get hot water for Callum's bath, so I needed firewood. Themba said, "You don't do that. The children have to do that." It was like a firm "You don't go up there at all. Only children go up there." There definitely is a line. You don't cross it. You don't go up the hill and fetch wood; that's what the children do.' It was also what daughters-in-law did, several times a week, but Lynn's incompetence at carrying the load home debarred her. After her first unsuccessful foray into the forest, she was neither asked nor volunteered again, but Daniel went several times, with the others. It was an adventure. The mountain was so much bigger than it looked, once you climbed a bit. You had to look for dying trees and cut them down. The amount of heavy timber that the girls carried on their heads amazed him.

Although Lynn acknowledged that with so many children in the homestead it was sensible to give them some of the work, she thought that the amount they worked their children was excessive. In her opinion, the adults of the homestead were very lazy. 'To justify the amount of work the children do, I'd have to see the adults doing a darned sight more.' She had come to Africa expecting to see the adults working very hard, but now that she was here she had completely revised her views. 'If you only look at bits of what the adults are doing, you do think they're working extraordinarily hard, but if you spend a whole day here, for several days, you realize the adult working day is a lot less than it is in England.'

In this she is almost certainly correct. Swazis value and preserve their leisure. Time is not money and they spend their time slowly, if they can. They pride themselves on the slow, dignified pace at which they walk and compare themselves favourably with scurrying foreigners. Only the people in paid employment get drawn into the hurried ways of the West. Lynn observed, 'Activity here is in bursts, very short bursts. Two hours here, two hours there. When they do it, it's hard physical work. But for the majority of time they don't work at all. And when the kids get home, they're doing everything that could have been done by adults during the day.' She called it 'child slave labour'. 'It's back to the days in England when boys went up chimneys. We've moved on from that. But they haven't moved on at all, over here.'

She remained convinced that children have more right to leisure than do adults, and was indignant that the homestead did not share her conviction. 'You don't see *make* and *babe* Shongwe up at four-thirty in the morning. You see the kids, doing the washing up, setting the fire, chopping wood. Then *make* Shongwe comes out and makes sour porridge – just a matter of putting it in the pot, stirring it and putting it on the fire – which has already been set… You can't justify this. Kids work flaming hard at school. Not just lessons. They have to cut the grass. They have to scrub the toilets on Fridays, despite the fact there's a school cleaner. Why do they need to scrub toilets at school? They're paying for their education.' (They are, of course, barely paying for their education at all. The amount that parents contribute, heavy burden though it is, is a mere token. One-quarter of the state's recurrent expenditure goes on education, the single biggest item in the budget.) 'When the children get in from school after that long – that huge – walk, they'll be out of

their uniforms setting the fire for dinner again, particularly if we are down in the fields doing one hour's weeding – and we've done nothing all day!' She continued self-righteously, 'If I was at home and I knew we were going to do weeding, I'd have done the dinner by now.'

Child labour was one of the aspects of Swazi society that Lynn refused to accept, even for ten weeks. 'The last few weeks it's been people getting used to my ways, as much as me getting used to their ways. I think it's now understood here that I don't work my own children and I don't work anybody else's. While I'm here I'm not going to do that, no matter how long I stay here.' It was not just the work that children did that troubled her. As far as she could see, they received no adult attention. Children did not come first. Inaccurately she observed, 'The only time people touch them around here is when they hit them, when they're in trouble.' She went on, 'I know it's a different culture, but I think children are a gift. You need to cherish them if you're going to turn them into decent human beings.' Warming to her theme she continued, 'I never see the children being praised. I never see the children being hugged. I never see the children being appreciated.' When they fell over, nobody picked them up.

ഗ

The Nestors linked child labour to corporal punishment. They believed that the Shongwe children submitted to this unfair regime only because if they did not, they would be hit. Lynn said, 'The children aren't doing it out of love, or even respect. They're doing it because they're frightened. If they do anything wrong, they're always beaten. I don't think it necessary to beat children into submission. I don't get it.'

Once again, her philosophy stood in stark contrast to that of *make* Shongwe, who said emphatically, 'If they are wrong I have to beat them.' She defended this as another traditional Swazi practice that toughened children for the hard life ahead. She had been beaten as a child, by her mother. She attributed her successful adult life to that experience: 'That's why I'm sitting in this homestead.' She was well aware that it was one of the traditions that was under attack by outsiders. Swaziland is a signatory to the United Nation's Declaration of the Rights of the Child. Her children had come home from school one day and told her that if she beat them, she would have to go to jail. 'I said, "Then let the [police] van come for me!"' She had no intention of stopping. 'In other countries their way is to leave children as they are, to do whatever they want, to rule their parents. My children have to learn the hard way. I think it's the right way. I may be wrong.'

In *make* Shongwe's opinion, not hitting children, women wearing trousers, electricity, computers and the taste for expensive things all belonged together in what she called 'civilization'. She saw it making its steady, insidious way into Swazi society through the schools. She predicted, 'Africa is going to end, because we are copying something that is not ours. We are copying other countries. That is why Africa is now finished.'

Lynn saw herself as a heroic agent of this very civilization. What she found 'really aggravating about this country' was that 'people will accept what is going on because it's the way it's always been'. She campaigned against dress codes for married women, against the sexual division of labour, against hierarchies of authority, against corporal punishment, against the Swazi child-rearing style, against leisurely Swazi work patterns. She did it in the name of progress.

ဆ Ꭷ

The day before they left the homestead for London, the Nestor children got back all the Western paraphernalia that had been taken from them on their first night at the hotel. Fighting broke out immediately. Lynn was dismayed. She said, 'I can't believe it. Within twelve hours they're fighting like cat and dog. Everything's back to normal. If I was staying, I'd burn the lot.' Instead they gave much of it away as farewell gifts to the homestead children. Their material legacy: some Western possessions and Robert's swing.

Once she had settled in, Chloe began to make friends with the Shongwe children.

CHAPTER TWELVE
getting cash

Nobody is sure just how much Swazi families rely on their land for a living. Experts have tried to measure the value of the goods that people enjoy from Nation Land: free water, free firewood, free grazing, free building materials of the traditional kind (poles, stones, sand, mud, thatch), free raw materials for making pots, baskets, sleeping mats and suchlike. They have tried to measure the value of the food produced and consumed on the homestead, but the sums are exceedingly difficult to compute and there is considerable argument about them.

For instance, although the Shongwes will each be able to tell you precisely how much dried maize they eventually store in their grain tanks in any year, none of them can tell you how much green maize they eat in any season, though on some days in 2001 they prepared eighty ears at one sitting. Nobody counts the pumpkins, tomatoes and onions that are picked daily from the garden. Nobody can begin to imagine how much *ligusha* is picked growing wild with the weeds. The firewood that the Shongwe children gather daily on the mountain is consciously valued. We know this, because the gas and paraffin stoves are used only when absolutely necessary; they cost money to run. But nobody thinks of firewood in terms of a particular sum of money saved, and the idea of paying for water strikes them as ludicrous.

What is less disputed is that, whatever the land supplies, it yields insufficient cash for contemporary life. Indeed, earning

(opposite)
Everybody is expected to earn money, somehow. Many women sell fruit and vegetables.

cash from the king's land has traditionally been disapproved of; the land is for people's use, not for making money. Where cash crops are grown on a large scale – cotton and tobacco, sugar, vegetables and pineapples – it is usually on designated sites as specially sanctioned community projects, subject to particular dispensations. Only a small minority of families earn significant cash from such a source. The Shongwes sell their limited surpluses of vegetables and occasionally maize. The sums are small, but they are part of a careful calculus by *make* Shongwe. In March she laboriously worked out her return on a bucketful of lettuces and twelve small bunches of bananas. With that money she would buy the raw ingredients for the cakes that she would make for the children to sell at school. *Babe* Shongwe said of his vegetables, 'People from around come and buy, and I take that money and buy a pack of chicken portions from Manzini, so that my children can have some variety in their food.'

Everybody on the homestead feels the obligation to raise some cash. Most women earn money from selling something – sometimes items they have made. *Make* Shongwe makes sugarless doughnuts, *vetkoeke*, which her children sell at school each week. She also sends them off to school with re-packaged, salted maize puffs, *emafohlofohlo*, a commercial product high in irresistible monosodium glutamate; like so many other Swazi women, she buys these in bulk in Manzini whenever anybody goes to town. Being mostly air and weighing next to nothing, they are easy to carry home.

The dragooning of children into selling is not the straightforward exploitation of child labour that it seems. It is part of their education. Marketing is seen as an essential skill for girls: as women, they will need to know how to

Firewood is free and valued, but this value is never consciously calculated.

raise cash for the many needs of their children. They must grasp the principles of investment, profit and re-investment. Money that comes into your pocket should be doubled by calculated investment before it is spent. *Make* Shongwe expects her children to start selling things at school when they are about ten, 'when they can count properly'. She herself was ten when her mother started teaching her. The first thing that her children do each day when they return from school is give an account of the day's trade and hand over the money, some of which they will receive the next day as their bus fare and dinner money. When *make* Shongwe was asked what she would do if she had a lot of money, her immediate response was not consumption but investment: she would build a shed and fill it with broilers for fattening for market.

Daniel, an old hand at trading Pokémon cards at school in London, needed no training in marketing. He was quick to exploit the Zombodze school market. As Lynn proudly said, 'He's sensed a good opportunity. What he does is, he'll go to the shop on the way to school and use his dinner money to buy twenty lollies at, say, three pence each. Then he'll sell them at five pence and come home with as much money as he started with, and he'll have had his lunch as well.' Another of his strategies was to 'buy up the whole stock of popcorn at two pence a throw. Then, because there's no popcorn at school – supply and demand – he knocks it out at five pence a time.' He was repeating a very old historical pattern. Very few Swazi children ever go to school with as much capital to invest as Daniel had each day.

Gogo laNkhosi was retailing fruit and vegetables, which she bought wholesale. However, Dokta's wife, laSibandze, scandalized the rest of the women of the homestead

In the summer children earn money for their families by picking guavas and selling them at the roadside.

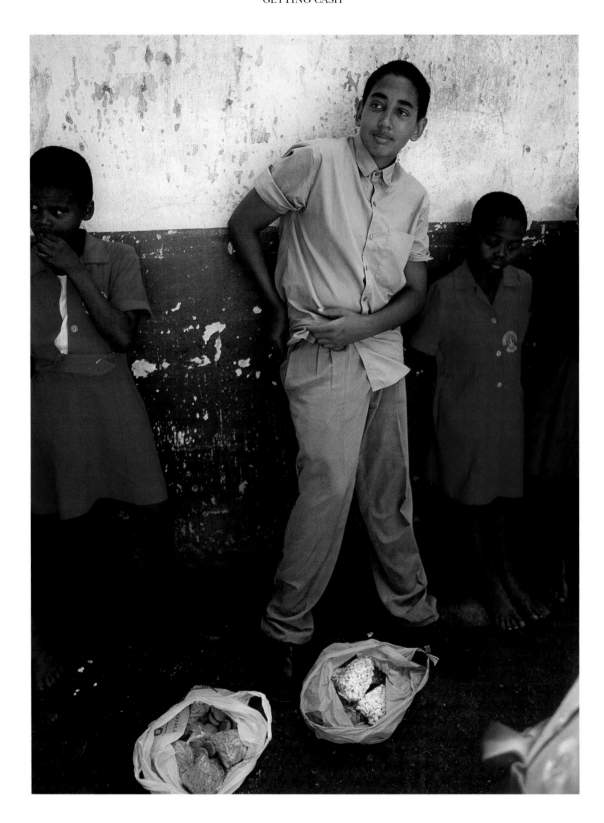

by selling nothing, while her children ran short of food. 'She must put a box on her head and go to work,' said *make* Shongwe. 'How can she just eat that small bit of money her husband gives her!'

Gogo laKhanyile makes and sells doormats from grass that she and her daughters and daughters-in-law gather on the mountain. Women's handiwork is poorly rewarded in the marketplace, but old women's options for making money are limited. They can also sell the grass itself to agents of a grass-weaving company who periodically pass by, looking for raw material. Sitting in the shade, apparently idly chatting, older women usually have a bundle of grass under one arm and a loop of plaited rope in their hands. This rope has many purposes around the homestead, from tethering goats and bundling firewood to holding down the thatch of the Great Hut.

The easiest way to get cash is to be in paid employment, but the supply of jobs falls far short of the demand. There was a brief boom in the 1980s, as entrepreneurs from South Africa, anxious to escape the sanctions against apartheid, crossed the border to gain access to markets denied them on political grounds. Since the 1990s many of them have relocated. Unemployment in

Gogo *laKhanyile (here with her grandchild Teme and* make *Shongwe) earns cash by making mats from grass.*

(opposite)
Daniel enjoyed the challenge of making money by wheeling and dealing at school.

Swaziland has been steadily growing as population growth exceeds economic growth. By the mid-1990s an estimated 54,000, one in six adults, were looking for work. When Robert joined them in February 2001, the proportion had certainly increased, probably to one in five, but nowhere near the '60 per cent' he claimed were looking.

The great majority of Swazi work-seekers find paid work in Swaziland, but some cross to South Africa – itself in no great economic shape at the start of the twenty-first century – traditionally to the mines, where employment is steadily shrinking. In 1998 fewer than 13,000 Swazis were working in the South African mines. Both of the unemployed men in the Shongwe homestead, Mandla and Dokta, were retrenched miners. In his halting English Dokta said, 'Last year I was working in the mine. There was no suffering last year. I leave the mine in August. Now I am starting suffering because I am not working. I have two children in the stage of going to school. There is no money for paying fees, there is no money for paying school funds. The only thing I have money for is exercise books. No money for books. No money for uniforms.' Once households have become dependent on a wage, its loss is devastating, but the effect is not immediate: the rural homestead, with its home-grown food and principle of sharing, can cushion the impact for several months.

Mandla thought it better to work in South Africa 'because you work eight hours a day. In Swaziland you are compelled to work more than eight hours.' This is true of some jobs in the timber plantations, the security industry and domestic service, but maximum hours, like minimum wages, are in fact laid down for each industry in Swaziland. They are also monitored, in most cases by vigorous trade unions.

Mandla's previous work had been in Swaziland, first thinning trees on the timber plantations that provide wood pulp to the paper industry in Japan, then as a machinist on one of the fly-by-night enterprises of southern Africa's textile industry. 'I operated five machines, making jerseys. I was awarded a certificate for that, but in 1991 the company closed down.'

In 2001 jerseys were once more being manufactured in Swaziland; one of *gogo* laKhanyile's daughters, Ngabisa, had just found work in such a factory within commuting distance of Ekudzeni, earning about twenty pounds a fortnight as a machinist. She was one of two women and six men of the homestead to be in paid work during the Nestors' stay.

There were thus eight sets of wages filtering back to the homestead at that time. Robert was quite incorrect in thinking that the money earned all went 'into a big pot'. In Swazi society money is a very personal matter. Each individual earner has a set of fluctuating obligations to certain other people, to whom discrete sums are given, privately. Everybody has a figurative purse or pocket in which their own money is kept. The earnings of the homestead's earners come back to the homestead in circuitous ways. *Umkhulu*, as homestead head, will receive a small sum from everyone, as a token of respect. Men give some money to the women who cook for them, some to their wives, some to the mothers of their children, some to the women who sleep with them, some to their fathers, some to their mothers. How much is given, and how often, depends on the circumstances in each instance.

When the Shongwes' herdsman needed to be paid, everybody was called to the Great Hut to discuss the matter. His monthly wages were overdue. Somebody had to pay him the fifteen pounds owed him. When Robert asked if they drew straws, they laughed and said no, it depended on people's pockets. Anybody who could find the money could report to *gogo* laKhanyile before Friday. Although the meeting had been pointedly translated into English for the Nestors' benefit, they sat tight. The herdsman had little to do with them; they were waiting to be asked to contribute to the common pot. A few days later Robert asked *make* Shongwe, 'When will I be asked to put forward my contribution to the home-stead?' He had already been asked and had missed his cue. -

ļ␣ ļ

Umkhulu has been continuously employed for nearly fifty years, ever since his father released him from cattle herding, when he was about eighteen. The most important purpose of a job then was to earn enough money to acquire cattle to marry. Swazi men still need cattle to marry, but they need cash for much else besides. In the past, marriage cattle were usually supplied by the family, but *umkhulu* was unlucky. 'When my father was still alive he instructed that, in respect of each of our sisters of the same mother, when the sister gets married and her in-laws pay cows for *lobolo*, those cows would be used to pay *lobolo* for each of the boys when they get married. Unfortunately for me, my sister's in-laws could not pay *lobolo* for marrying her. That meant I had to struggle on my own.'

His first job in the early 1950s was on a poultry farm about twenty miles from Ekudzeni, belonging to an English settler. On the farm young Shongwe learnt how to construct a road, how to use a pick and how to hatch chicks in an incubator. He was paid about ten pounds a month. At that time cattle could be bought for about twenty pounds each. Militant workers were campaigning to be paid a pound a day, but *umkhulu* was young and did not expect a man's wage. He was provided with rations and a dilapidated room, which he shared with a fellow labourer.

He has always found work with quarters, and has consequently lived in many different places with changing jobs, always returning to Ekudzeni at the week's or month's end. For many years he worked as a security guard, first for a bus owner, then for a timber company and finally as supervisor in a security company, where, to his horror, 'We were given guns to use while providing security for this car, which had to transport money to pay wages. We prayed that we would not encounter a situation where we would be required to shoot. We used to pray, even for the person who had planned the attack, that he would not do so.' As a groundsman for one of the government ministries, his current work is to keep the vigorous indigenous grass looking like a lawn.

Gogo laBhembe is one of two women of the homestead in current waged employment. She has not always been in paid work. Until about eight years ago she lived at Ekudzeni, cultivating her fields, cooking for the children, fetching water from the stream with the other wives and daughters-in-law (there was no tapped water in those days). In 1993, driven in part by polygamous marital disharmony and by fear (she had lost children at birth), but also by economic pressure, she decided to return to her maternal grandfather's home in Mbabane and find work there. 'My husband had many wives, and at his place of work he earned a low wage. He could not meet the needs of all his households.' She remembered the children at the homestead having inadequate clothes in cold weather and no shoes. 'It made me hurt to see the children struggling that way.'

She found work as a domestic servant, a job she had done years before, when, aged fourteen and forced out of school by poverty, she had worked for a Mrs Zulu. She recalls, 'I earned four *emalangeni* [less than two pounds in 1970] a month. I used to give three to my mother and I kept one for myself.' This time, after several false starts, she found work with the Simelane family in Mbabane. Domestic service can have many advantages if the house you are working for is a rich one. Food is likely to be plentiful and the opportunities to help yourself to it frequent. When housing is provided, the hours are invariably long,

however, and the cash rewards disproportionately low.

Gogo laBhembe lived out. She was paid about thirty pounds a month, of which a quarter went to the nursemaid whom she paid to look after her new baby. She was one of several employed staff. Although her wages were steadily increased to just over fifty pounds a month during the next five years, her hours remained very rigid. She worked a six-day week. 'I was not even allowed to attend funerals at my husband's home.'

In 2000 she was pleased to find alternative work in a noisy warren of small shops near the bus rank in Mbabane, where she does some cleaning and takes money from people using the lavatory. 'This job is better. For the past years I did not get time to go to my husband's home and perform my duties as a wife, but now I get time to go home.' She goes back to the homestead very occasionally. The Nestors were almost oblivious of her existence, though they came to know her sons quite well, assuming that they were *gogo* laKhanyile's. *Gogo* laBhembe does get to the homestead more often during the ploughing season. 'When there is a lot of weeding I go home to weed. On holidays I also go, and during the time for harvesting. If there is something urgent that requires me, I simply shoot home. In my previous work I didn't have off-days.'

Umkhulu had four sons in work in 2001. Amos, his firstborn, works as a labourer for the government and gets home at least once a month. His wife, Thandi laMabuza, visits him frequently at work during the winter months when the homestead agricultural tasks are over. *Gogo* laKhanyile's firstborn, Sipho, is a miner in South Africa. His wife lives at Ekudzeni, and they see him twice a year. Two more of her sons, Simon and

Mavela, have labouring jobs in Swaziland. Simon's wife lives on the homestead. Mavela, who has just started work in Mbabane, shares *umkhulu*'s government quarters.

Babe Shongwe is a policeman who escorts the prime minister. It was he who took his annual leave to be on the homestead for six weeks of the Nestors' nine-week stay. It was quite a shock for them to see him loading his service pistol the night that he returned to work. He had seemed such a farmer. It was hard to imagine him wearing polished boots and buttons and saluting to the mighty. At work he shares quarters in Mbabane, and gets home at least once every three weeks.

As the Shongwes demonstrate, it is very difficult to stay at Ekudzeni once you are in work. Like most rural Swazis, they have no option but to resign themselves to a system whereby, while some stay at home to grow food and tend the children and cattle, others must live away in order to earn a wage. The arrangement does not strike them as particularly outrageous. The homestead is not couple-centred as in the West, but is a bigger persisting community bound by descent. When *babe* Shongwe went back to work *make* Shongwe said, 'I won't miss him because I'm used to doing the work and we need the money.'

Mats from plaited knotted grass, like this one, are not traditional items but are specially made to sell to whites from South Africa.

(opposite)
Gogo *laBhembe*, one of umkhulu's *wives, outside the half-finished house she is building herself in Mbabane, where she lives and works as a cleaner.*

CHAPTER THIRTEEN
robert joins the workforce

From the outset Robert found African rural life much easier and more pleasant than Lynn did. He liked the clean air, and the quiet road on which he could take his morning jog. He liked the river where the Shongwe children swim and joined them exuberantly, unaware of the unwritten expectation that the grown men of the homestead do not swim with its young girls. He appreciated the hospitality that his family was being offered. 'We came here with nothing, basically, and they have looked after us. They've fed us and they've not asked for nothing in return. There's not a lot of places you can actually go around the world, and people will treat you like that. So I appreciate the way we've been treated and the mutual respect that we've got. They've welcomed us with open arms.'

Robert found other men and boys in the homestead willing to share in his passion for exercise. 'What I've found to be common ground is exercise – giving them exercise in the morning for an hour. That is one barrier I have managed to break down and make some sort of connection with them.' But at the end of his first fortnight he felt he had plumbed the depths of any possible intimacy. He had not made friends. 'I talk to everybody, but it's just general chitchat, things about the homestead, what they're doing today; it's only about what's going on within this compound. I don't actually talk about anything else. There's that part of my life they don't

(opposite)
For a week in Swaziland Robert worked as 'Ronnie' serving iced drinks to golfers at a five-star hotel.

*While in Africa, Robert
trained by himself every
day: jogging, skipping
and shadow boxing.*

know about.' He went on, 'There hasn't been a lot of common
ground. The work they do is totally different from the work I do.
The way they think is totally different. Between us and the homestead there is a mutual understanding that we have a conversation
out of politeness. The people here are not educated, but they've
got very good manners.'

Robert claimed not to mind about this, 'I'm not really sociable, like Lynn. She does like having a lot of people around her all
the time. Being here does seem to drive her up the wall a bit.'

But Lynn thought Robert minded more than he let on. The
novelty of being on the homestead was wearing thin after two
weeks. He was spending his evenings with her, rather than with
the men down at the men's enclosure. 'There's nothing much for
him to do unless he hangs out with the lads. Rob's idea of hanging out is to have some beers and talk about football, but there's
not much of that here.'

When Robert decided that, like other men of the homestead, he needed to find paid work, he viewed with alarm the
prospect of being separated from his wife and children. 'That
isn't the way our family works,' he correctly observed. 'Daniel's
reaching the age where he needs discipline and I can't leave

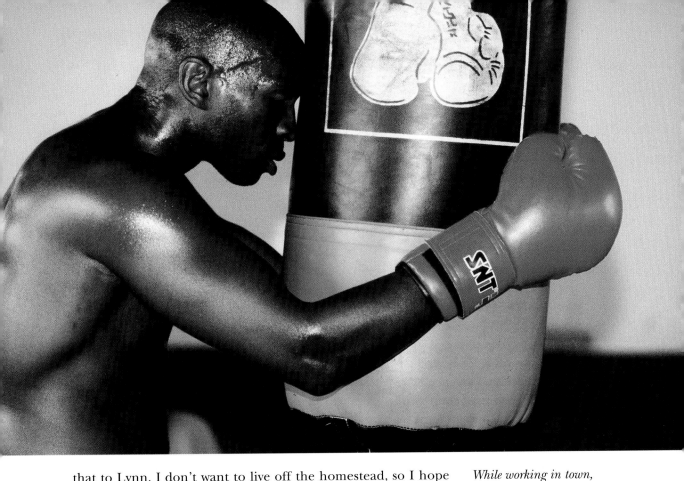

that to Lynn. I don't want to live off the homestead, so I hope I'll be able to cope with the travelling. I want to get back to my kids and my missus to make sure they're OK. That's how I want to work. That's what I'm used to.' And there were other considerations. He saw that, as a stranger, he would find it hard to get cheap accommodation elsewhere; he had no relatives to draw on. He was unlikely to find a job that paid enough to afford strangers' accommodation. Because he wanted to come home each night, he needed to find work close at hand or the journey would be too taxing. 'I'm not going to travel outside Manzini to get a job. I don't see the point, to be quite honest, busting my arse to get there.' Optimistically he set out with unemployed Dokta to look for work close to home.

He was confident he would get a job. He had often looked for work in London. He said, 'I'll bullshit my way in.' He claimed not to mind what he did, as long as it brought in some money. 'We're down to our last twenty pounds, enough to last a single person a couple of days. Hopefully I'll be lucky.' He was not the sort of person who gave up easily. 'I'll keep trying. If I don't get one, it's down to people not recognizing good talent when they see it.'

While working in town, Robert managed to find somewhere to indulge his passion.

Lynn was equally confident. 'He's never been out of work more than three or four days. At home he always manages to get something. He just walks the streets till he finds something. As long as he can feed the children.'

Make Shongwe brought them up sharp. It was not just a question of feeding his own children. 'If you are a man you have to look after the whole family. I have to share the money I get from *babe* Shongwe with everybody, even *gogo*. It's very important for *everybody* that you and Dokta look for a job. Things are very expensive.' She warned that it would not be easy. 'They keep promising you to come back, come back. They don't tell you the truth, that there's no vacancy.' Their best chance lay on the new road construction site, not far from Ekudzeni , where local residents were being given preference.

It was exactly as *make* Shongwe had predicted. The foreman at the site said that they definitely needed some people in a week or two. 'We take from the site. You're expected to come every morning at seven, to see if there's a job available. Keep checking.' He could not guarantee employment.

Robert was indignant. 'I've got to get up at five and get a bus to be down here at seven so that he can tell me he hasn't got a job for me? I'm not doing that!' He turned to Dokta. 'I don't know if you want to get up at five o' clock in the morning to be rejected, because that's what it is. I'm not good at rejection. I don't do it good and I don't like it. I'm not gonna do it.'

Dokta's response was stoical. He could not afford to ignore any job possibility. He agreed that it was difficult to get up in the morning and be rejected, 'But I can do it because I just want a job. Maybe in two weeks coming there's going to be a job for labourers.'

Robert thought Dokta's passive acceptance of the situation was tragic. 'The people who live in this country have to bring themselves down to a certain level to get themselves a job. I think that's just ridiculous. I feel for Dokta, because I know he will get up and go to that guy, and the guy'll say, "Sorry, I haven't got a job for you." I know he's going to do that for a few weeks. It's the Swazi way, but I'm not a Swazi, so I refuse to do it. I refuse to conform to their way of doing things.' He would look elsewhere, where people would offer him something positive, and not just a carrot dangling from the end of a stick. 'We might have something tomorrow – that's not good enough for me! I don't deal in shallow promises.'

After several days of tramping the industrial areas with Dokta and seldom getting beyond the security fences. After hours of waiting in the sun trying vainly to wrest names and telephone numbers of managers and personnel officers from unsympathetic gatekeepers, Robert was frustrated by their search. He thought he knew the ropes but, not knowing siSwati, he had to rely on Dokta to speak for them both. Robert remarked, 'In England if I went to a factory I'd at least get past the security guard to the receptionist. Here the people at the gate are there to fob off people like me who want a job.' Dokta had theories about their lack of success. Jobs were being reserved by the management for foreigners, and for workers' relatives by other employees further down the line. This was almost certainly true. A reference from a reliable worker about one of his relatives carries as much weight as anything else, and family authority can then be manipulated to the firm's advantage.

ଯ ଓ

There was something else on Dokta's mind; his unfriendly reception at the factory gates could not be put down just to chance.
Somebody was sending him bad luck. Perhaps some jealous
person had bewitched him. Perhaps he had brought it on himself
by displeasing his dead father in some way. He needed a diagnosis. He had to cleanse himself of this bad luck. He needed to
consult a healer.

Swazi traditional healers draw no sharp distinction between
physical and social problems. All problems can be attributed
either to ancestral displeasure or to *batakatsi*, witches and evil-
doers, the embodiment of jealousy. It is the healer's job to make
the appropriate diagnosis and to prescribe what must be done.
An advertisement in the local paper from a visiting quack hoping
to break into this market gives the flavour. He lists the ailments
he is able to cure:

TB, skin problems, heart pains, asthma, diarrhoea, kidneys, bad spirit,
woman not getting children, couples' problems, bad luck to throw away
demons, stomach aches, headache, coughs, paralysis, blood shortage,
give luck to schoolchildren, toothache, thieves' problems.

Traditional medicine is big
business in Swaziland. Here
is a market stall well stocked
with herbal remedies.

But Swazis have no need to rely on foreign practitioners; the country is already over-supplied with people who have either been called by their ancestors to heal or have simply learnt their skills through apprenticeship.

Robert was sceptical. He had little time for what he saw as hocus-pocus, but he was persuaded to accompany Dokta one after-noon to consult a recommended woman diviner, a *sangoma* who worked with bones and spirits. Dokta's brother Themba and *make* Shongwe went too. If Themba's ancestors were going to speak, he wanted to be there to hear them. He said, 'I believe in my ancestors very much.' The group was led into a small pink-walled hut where the assistants and apprentices were already seated, bare-footed, about the walls, waiting to sing and drum and rattle tins of small stones.

Robert did not enjoy the experience, as the diviner – with her ochred red hair, her cowrie-shell anklets and chattering teeth – conveyed, like a ventriloquist, in the hoarse staccato tones of the long-departed, messages from the shades, accompanied by furious drumming and singing by her assistants. After his first cautious throw of the bones – augmented by a small mosaic tile and a coin – he chose not to participate in the ritual.

The Shongwes took part with practised enthusiasm as, piece by piece, the *sangoma* correctly outlined Dokta's problem: an inabil-ity to find work. '*Siyavuma*,' they chanted, '*Siyavuma*, we agree.' Robert watched the Shongwes conspicuously place her fee, a bundle of banknotes, under her grass mat. As the drumming increased he watched her change her clothes, while Dokta stripped to the waist and sat on the mat, ready to submit to her ministrations. In a trance she blew on him and brushed him gently from top to toe

with her traditional whisk made from an animal's tail. Now possessed by her ancestors, and talking to his, she shook convulsively, she trembled, she sweated, she gasped, she grimaced. She changed her wig, she changed her voice. She blew into his ears, pummelled on his shoulders and shook his arms. Eventually she prescribed medicines: one to take, one to bath in.

Dokta felt strengthened and optimistic. Robert felt nothing; he was pleased when it was over. 'It shows me the other side of what it's actually like to be African. This is Africa raw, not like I am, watered down. I feel totally separate from it. It's not the way I was brought up. Sometimes there's a brief glimpse and I feel part of it. Other times I feel like a tourist. I wasn't born in Africa. I can see it, but I'll never live it.'

ඊ ෆ

At the end of February Robert and Dokta found temporary work as casual labourers at Swaziland's most expensive hotel for the dura-tion of a regional golf tournament. Dokta was to work in the kitchen, washing and polishing plates, glasses and cutlery. Robert was to man one of the many refreshment points on the golf course, where thirsty players could get iced water and fruit. Later he might be trained for work in the dining room. They would earn about thirty-four pence an hour and be given one free meal for an eight-hour shift. They were to report on Monday morning at six, wearing black trousers and black shoes. An ethnic-print shirt would be provided. Robert said wryly, 'I'm off to find my black trousers and my subservient attitude.'

Since their shift started at six in the morn-ing, they would need to find local accommo-dation. Dokta said they could share *umkhulu*'s

Dokta learning to fold table napkins at the hotel.

room in Mbabane for a week. 'We don't need nothing posh,' said Robert. 'Just a mat on the floor.' He had underestimated the privations of the homestead's migrant workers. *Umkhulu*'s room was small and bleak, with a concrete floor, a single overhead bulb and a single bed. Two of Dokta's brothers were already sharing the room with their father. It was difficult to manoeuvre to provide sufficient space for them all to lie down on the floor at the same time. Robert was unfazed. 'It's not a big shock. I can deal with this. It's better than sleeping outside.' The Shongwes, father and three sons, soon settled down, but Robert could not sleep. The floor was hard and he was within walking distance of a city centre at last. He crept out and made his way into the town to 'chill out'.

By the following night Dokta had found a neighbour working in the hotel who, for four pounds, would rent them a room for the week in his nearby house. 'He's got electricity, shower, everything,' Dokta said proudly. Robert would miss the bright lights of Mbabane, but they would save time and bus fares. The room was furnished with a sideboard and a double bed. Dokta, accustomed to inadequate urban space, assumed that they could share the bed, but Robert was adamant. 'I don't want to sleep in that bed with you, Dokta! The only person I sleep with is my flipping missus! Ask him for another mattress or something. He's your mate. I want to get myself sorted.' Which he did. He slept, alone, on the double bed. Dokta slept on the floor.

The uneven relationship between the talk-ative, assertive Robert and the unassuming, passive Dokta underwent a subtle shift during the next week. Dokta might have seemed unenterprising in his search for a job, but once in work, he was a good worker. He aimed to please by doing well everything that was required of him. A Swazi man working with other Swazi men, he felt comfortable and compared to the mines, the hotel was sheer luxury. There was no danger of falling rocks, no stomach-lurching descent in a crowded cage. The workers' canteen was like a restau-rant he had glimpsed but never entered and the food was free and limitless. The manage-ment noted his attitude with approval and at the end of the week they put him on their permanent roster of casual workers.

By contrast, Robert entered work as into battle, fighting every inch of the way. Since workers were everywhere exploited, it was their duty to take advantage of every little opportunity that the workplace offered. 'I can't see myself working here for the next six weeks. I'm having trouble doing it for a day. It's the vibes. They're all here to serve people. That's the bit I don't like. This is the lowest I will go to earn a living.' He worked the system. He found out where to get a hot shower, and showered. He got the hotel laun-dry service to wash and dry his clothes. He

openly ate the fruit from his kiosk that was intended for the golfers. He persuaded the staff in the canteen to bring him breakfast when everyone else had eaten and the coun-ters had been cleared for lunch. He refused to hurry when the manager sent for him, 'The manager will have to wait till I've had something to eat.' When his manager failed, mid-morning, to bring Robert the sandwich he had asked for, he got angry. 'That put my back up.' He demanded that he be given the best lunch slot: 'If Elias had brought me a sandwich, I'd be all right. All I had was two flipping bread rolls and some jam and orange juice and fruit. So I'm going to take my lunch at twelve.' It was a matter of princi-ple. 'You've got to look after your staff, man. He should bring them some food; treat them better than that.'

By the second day his resentment had melted a little under the benign hotel regime. He commented, 'I'd rather be stuck out here doing this than be stuck in a ware-house. When it comes down to survival, you can't be picky and choosy. Living here is not easy. You have to bite your tongue and humble yourself. The only thing that makes it easy for me is that it's not for good.' It was in this cool frame of mind that he invented Ronnie. Ronnie was the name tag that the hotel had pinned on him from day one. It was company policy that every employee had a name tag. Casuals had to take whatever name they were given. As Robert observed, 'They don't care what you're called.' So, for a few hours, playfully distancing himself from his menial work, Robert became Ronnie. Ronnie spoke English with a Swazi accent. He was subservient. As long as he was Ronnie, he did not mind being deferential. He did not mind saying, 'OK, sir! Enjoy, sir! Sorry, madam!' It was an ingenious way of coping with the management's expectations. 'If I'm just messing about, I can do it. If I'm serious, it just sticks in my throat and it won't come out.'

Ronnie did not last long. At first his manager thought he must be misunderstanding what was required. Swazis pride themselves on the respect they show one another. They are extravagantly polite to each other. They commonly greet one another as *nkhosi*, lord, or *umnumzane*, sir. They have little difficulty extending this courtesy to others and little understanding of the resentment that similar terms can evoke among people with a different history and experience. Patiently the manager explained to Robert, 'As you take the plate you say, "Thank you, sir. Thank you, madam."'

Robert replied, 'I've never said "sir" in my life, so I don't say it now – sorry.'

The manager tried again. 'When you put the teapot on the table you say, "Here is the tea, sir. Here is the tea, sir." Remember that. I want to hear you say it. Now, let us go together and serve those gentlemen.' Which they did.

Robert, obstinately and heroically, said, 'Hello, my man. Here is your tea.' They moved him to the kitchen to wash plates with Dokta.

A day later Robert was asked at short notice if he would do a double shift. This too he refused on principle. He complained, 'There's no sort of pleading in the way they ask you. They command you. It's not a request. It's like: you have to do this!' He asked fellow workers whether they took on double shifts without due notice. They did, often. One of them explained, 'There's nothing I can say. I must. I ask for a job, he gives me a job, and now I don't want to work!

They're going to pay me overtime. They command you.'

Robert understood their position and pitied them. 'They have no choice. They're only here for the money. They're not racially oppressed. They're financially oppressed, giving them a subservient attitude to people in charge. People are being held back by their own people.'

While he was working at the hotel, Robert nonchalantly turned down an opportunity to see the Swazi king, who was to attend a banquet to honour the visiting vice-president of South Africa. His decision astounded his Swazi fellow workers, who were excited by the forthcoming visit and manoeuvring for the privilege of being close to the king.

The Nestors, fresh from Cool Britannia, where the royal family is fair game for every newspaper writer and comedian, had no idea of the very different way in which the Swazi royal family is regarded. Robert had no conception of the privilege he was being afforded when the management of the hotel at which he was working for a week offered him the chance to be on duty at the dinner attended by the king and the vice-president of South Africa. Would he be interested?

'I doubt it,' said Robert loftily. 'I'm on my way to see my family. I'd rather spend some quality time with my kids and my wife.'

It was a complex clash of ideologies: on the one hand, the white hotel manager, going local, taking for granted the contagious glamour of blacks in high political office – the king in particular; on the other, the black British working man, with studied indifference to the local social order, self-righteously putting his family first. Robert was striking a blow for Everyman. 'I'm not into politicians,' he said dismissively. 'Whatever country they run their

Caddies below; golfers and their guests above. Robert found that he needed a 'subservient attitude' to get by as a worker in this hotel.

mouth is just full of bullshit.' There was another dimension to the clash: worker versus employer. Robert's rejection overstepped local norms; employees did not reject opportunities to do over-time, especially prestigious work like this. The manager felt the rebuff. In a measured tone he said, 'OK, there are three hundred people waiting outside the door. We'll take one of them.'

Robert was elated by his decision. He saw no kudos in meet-ing the king. 'When I got home half the people would say to me, "Who the hell is the king of Swaziland?" I wish him all the luck in the world and I hope he's a good king and sorts his country out.'

Robert did not immediately return to his family, as he had so loftily suggested. He paid a caddie about three pounds and, in the misty rain, had his first golf lesson on the greens used by the champions.

After a week at the hotel Robert said, 'I've had to learn to be a bit civil to people. It's been a good experience. I'm not a waiter at heart.' He was already looking forward to the start of the following week. He had been half-promised work in a security firm by a retired British Army officer he had met. Optimistically he said to Dokta, 'Security work is better than this. There's a bit more freedom. And the money will be better than we get here.'

'You'll have to say "sir" to the captain,' Dokta warned him. 'You'll have to salute like soldiers.'

Robert was confident there would be no such pressure. The boss was from England; Robert called him by his first name. But if there was such a requirement, he would refuse. 'It's not the flaming Army, is it? It's a tin-pot security firm. I ain't doing it.'

Dokta was adamant. 'The way I'm telling you is the truth. Here in Swaziland they call each other "sir". He will give you some rules.'

There were indeed rules. Robert heard them the next week. They were briskly delivered, military-style, over the retired Army officer's desk, while Dokta waited outside. Robert was to help guard the residence of a major client. 'You'll fit in till you open your mouth. Know what I mean? You'll be casual, not permanent. I could lay you off at any time, you do understand that? If you're still with me at the end of the week, I'll pay you then.' Robert was too intimidated to ask how much he would be paid. But he did ask if there was any work for Dokta. This was clearly an impertinence. 'People don't just walk in my door and ask for work.' He had made an exception for Robert as a fellow national. Dokta could take the Swazi route and talk to the man at the gate.

There was one more thing. 'It's very unlikely you'll meet my client. He drives a white Mercedes. But if perchance you see

him, greet him. You've probably experienced it already: in this part of the world people greet each other more than they do back in the UK. Greet him nicely, with a smile on your face. I'm not wanting to get all militarified, but have a little bit of bearing about yourself. Stand up a little bit. Be professional and a bit smart. "Good morning, Mr Bilbrough. How are you, sir?" Got any problem with that?'

Robert had a problem. 'I'm not ready to call people "sir".'

'Let me tell you,' said the retired Army officer impatiently, 'it goes with the job. It shouldn't cause you a problem.' Robert was to report the next day to get his uniform and meet the inspector. 'Esau, a good man. Came through the ranks.'

Robert said, 'Thank you for the opportunity.' But he did not take it. It was quite impractical. He would not be able to get to Manzini by half-past five in the morning. There were no buses at that hour. The rate of pay was worse than it was at the hotel. Dokta had discovered that from the man at the gate. Less than twenty-five pence an hour; less than three pounds a day. No boundless hotel meals. And he would be expected to say 'sir'.

He did not look for work in Swaziland again. The unemployment rate discouraged him. The logistics defeated him. Anyway, the homestead would support him. He was *umkhulu*'s son. There was an additional factor: Lynn. She was increasingly frustrated by the confines of the homestead and thought Robert was having all the fun. What she wanted was role-reversal. Let Robert stay on the homestead with the children for the rest of their stay,, and she would try her hand at finding a job.

CHAPTER FOURTEEN
women's work

Lynn sorely missed her London social life. 'England is just so far removed. Nobody here has been there, or knows anything about it. They haven't a clue.' More distressing than their ignorance about her life in London was the Shongwes' complete lack of curiosity about it.

The Nestors had assumed that people in Africa would be curious about the world they came from. Robert had said, 'I'd like to hear their views on how they think we live in London.' He told Chloe, 'They're gonna want to know what your school's like over here.' Lynn said that she thought they would be the source of great local curiosity. Instead there was simply indifference. Daniel's teacher displayed it when correcting his work one day. Daniel had used South African rather than Swazi currency in his answer.

'Where do you come from?' she asked him.

'London,' said Daniel.

'Do you use dollars there?'

'No,' said Daniel, surprised. 'We use pounds and pence.'

'Here we use *emalangeni*,' she said, 'Remember that.'

The Western assumption that it has so much to teach Africa was in a head-on confrontation with an African assumption that, at least in this situation, the Westerners were the ones in need of instruction. 'They never ask any questions,' said Lynn. 'If I ask them questions, they'll answer me, you know, quite

(opposite)
Lynn and Chloe fighting
red mud after rain.

Tapped water in the homestead meant Lynn did not have to go far to wash dishes or clothes.

fully. They're more than willing to tell you, you can tell that. But *they* never ask *me!*'

Lynn missed her telephone chats. She missed being able to 'nip down the road in the car to do some shopping' or to 'pop over to a friend'. 'This would do my head in: the very fact that people don't drop in; that you can't drop in on people without walking three hours up a mountain.' When, in her fifth week, she accompanied *gogo* laNkhosi on her rounds as rural health motivator and met some chronically ill neighbours, Lynn remarked with relief, 'At last I've got somewhere to pop into now. I can take the kids too.'

The language barrier was acute. Conversationally, she felt restricted to *make* Shongwe and the company of the few homestead adolescents who had survived school long enough to master some rudimentary English. Although she was able to have 'quite a laugh' with *make* Shongwe, there was little intimacy. 'I ask her a question and she tells me, and I tell her how it is at home. But as for making a close friend, I don't think so. I could never be close friends with anybody here.' She missed the familiar terms with which, in her social circles, the gender war was waged: there was none of what she called the 'girlie level of conversation'. 'I've never heard *make* Shongwe say anything bad about *babe* Shongwe.' She missed being able to gossip. 'There's nothing to gossip about.'

Unable to join in the homestead's conversations, Lynn found herself unable even to imagine what the women talked about when they gathered in the evenings on the kitchen steps. 'By the end of ten weeks I might sit out there some nights. I haven't done so yet. I couldn't bring myself to sit out there. I don't know what they find to talk about. Such a close community all the time. I mean, what *do* they talk about?'

Daniel sympathized with her. 'Everybody just sits around, chatter, chatter chatter in siSwati, so my mum can't join in with them.' Of course, they talked about Lynn quite a lot of the time, while she lay on the bed and read and smoked.

They thought her behaviour odd. They talked about the way she waited on her children and the way she did not join in. She was always indoors. Even on the few days that she cooked, she did not sit outside and prepare the food with the others. She cut potatoes up by herself, privately, in her room. She emerged only to put the food on the fire. The only time they saw her was when she was getting water at the tap or doing her washing. That washing! They had never seen so much. And she did it so badly, hanging up clothes still stained red with earth. Xolile said they bathed in the same basin they used for dishes: bodies and dishes, all mixed up, body fluids and food. It was dangerous. People could become ill.

After four consecutive days on the homestead without Robert, who was sleeping over at his hotel job, Lynn confessed herself 'bored witless'. She was, she said, 'climbing the walls. If I don't get out I'm going to murder my children.' Afterwards she defined this as a period of clinical depression and insanity. Afterwards

she remarked, 'I've become really good friends with *make* Shongwe and with Thandi.' And they were lasting friendships, because she had worked so hard at them, not like the boyish 'here today, gone tomorrow' friendships that came so easily to Robert. Afterwards she said she wished that she had not taken so long to settle down. It was her one regret, but quite understandable. She had had to put up with so much more adjusting. Robert's life on the homestead was not so very different from his life in London.

Lynn had grown up as ideas of women's emancipation from domestic labour took hold in Britain. Her own mother was a full-time housewife, but Lynn entered marriage as a 1980s' superwoman: someone who could do everything and hold down a full-time job. For ten years she ran around 'like a headless chicken – cooking, cleaning, washing, ironing, looking after kids, picking up kids, dropping off kids, dinner on the table'. Then she delivered an ultimatum to Robert: he must help with all the domestic tasks or get out. Robert realized that she was serious, and started to share the childcare and the housework.

The notion that the emancipation of women means freedom to earn, like men, is peculiar to the West, the consequence of women's steady economic marginalization as the industrialized economy matured. Women tend to shun domestic work at home as a symbol of their former enslavement. Men tend to shun it as something they could well go on doing without. Fast food, microwave ovens, washing machines, charladies, cheap restaurants, au pairs, childminders and crèches all help to ensure that nobody does as much of their own domestic work as their grandmothers did. But domestic work refuses to disappear. It continues to be a battleground

A wheelbarrow serves as a portable sink for the Shongwes.

between the sexes for the Nestors, as in many other British households.

The situation in Africa is quite different. African women have never been economically marginalized. Although intrusive Western economic institutions have viewed men rather than women as the main wage-earners, and have employed them accordingly, the transition to a Western-style industrial economy is so puny, so incomplete, even in the industrialized south, that other sources of economic power – such as food and handicraft production, and marketing – still provide women with a base for an enviable leverage and independence. Any subservience to men is formal and ideological rather than structural. The contrast between Britain and Swaziland is quite sharp in this respect. In Britain, the ideology is equality; the reality is that women have control over far fewer resources than men. In Swaziland, the ideology is that men dominate; the reality is that women have considerable economic power – as they always have had.

Lynn had, properly, anticipated a clear division of work in Africa between men and women. But she misunderstood how important women's work was. She thought of it as housewifery. Before she left she said, 'If my role over there is to be at home, that's fine. I quite enjoy being a housewife when I get the chance. It should be a rest, really. In Africa everybody knows what they have to do. Women are quite content in their roles. It's something I look forward to.' She misjudged herself. The women certainly knew what they had to do, and they were apparently content with their role. It was this very contentment that riled her. 'Nobody seems to want to change. I don't see any signs of rebellion. They're all quite happy.'

She was not at all happy. She had not grasped the important difference in Africa between being at home and being a housewife. Home, the homestead, is a place where important economic activities take place. Food is planted, fertilized, weeded, harvested, stored, processed, not just cooked. Water is fetched, carried, warmed, not just turned on. Fuel has to be found, chopped down, carried, broken up, ignited, not just switched on. Meat as livestock has to be housed or herded, fed, doctored when ill, slaughtered, butchered, not just roasted. When the roof leaks you do not call a builder. The Shongwes called a grandmother to ask whether she had picked and prepared the grass the previous winter. They called the herdsman and asked him to fetch the oxen down from the mountain and make ready the sledge to fetch the grass from grandmother's house. They called a brother to make a ladder, and he went on to the mountain and found and cut down straight saplings for the job. They asked their daughters if they had plaited the rope. The work team came together after long preparations.

Women do a lot of this home work because they usually are at home, because they are responsible for the food and children. Besides this, they organize the laundry, and the tidying and cleaning of the houses, go to the shops to buy the goods they can neither make nor do without, and plan how to make money by selling something at a profit.

Lynn settled down, instead, to being just a housewife. Contrary to her optimistic expectations in London, she did not enjoy it. Once the novelty of doing the family washing out in the open by the tap had worn off, she readily succumbed to the homestead's definition of herself as an inefficient laundress, and allowed the other women to take over the difficult bits – the soiled white socks, the soiled white shorts. One day Themba's brother Mandla did Lynn's washing for her. To ribald mockery from the women, he hung up her underwear on the line, complaining that he had been bewitched; somebody had put a love potion in his food. Lynn's inability to wash her children's clothes clean remained a source of jocular comment throughout their stay. When Xolile washed something badly the women said, 'You are getting like your mother!' After some initial dismay at her own incompetence, Lynn entered into the joke, complaining that Thandi laMabuza 'mugged' her for her washing.

She also let others take over the cleaning of the floors of the two rooms they had been allocated. She had never had to clean a concrete floor before. Xolile and Thandi laMabuza each demonstrated the way, on their hands and knees, first using a bucket of soapy water and a cloth, then a tin of polish and a brush. It was hard work. Lynn was happy to watch them. Thandi said, 'When I started assisting them I did not intend that they should relax and do nothing.' But as she saw the Nestors' room sink into potential squalor, she felt she had to keep cleaning it. She confessed to enjoying this chore. She got into the routine of going to help Lynn with her housework every day. Thandi liked both Lynn and Robert. She found them an amusing diversion and said she would be lonely when they left. As for their children, she said, 'I love them, but they are difficult to cope with. They don't take their shoes off in the house, even while I am washing the floor. If I had to live with them for long I would be tempted to hit them.'

Lynn did not hit them, but she found their 'twenty-four by seven' company wearying. 'There are only so many card games you

Thandi laMabuza renews her doorstep with fresh cow dung.

*The rains fall in Swaziland in the summer, sometimes in
dazzling electrical storms, sometimes in dreary day-long drizzle.*

can play with Snap cards.' It was especially tiresome when it rained. The yard became wet and slippery, the roof leaked and the room filled with mud and wet washing. Home school, Nestor-style, obliged them all to spend some hours together in the room each morning, with the children perched on the bed, writing and drawing, while Lynn tried to read a novel. Sometimes when it was Robert's rare turn, he fell asleep, much to Chloe's annoyance. He defended himself, 'Sleeping or lying down reading a book – what's the difference?'

There was no doubt that Lynn was becoming intensely bored. 'With a house this size there's only so much housework you can do.' She also remarked, 'When did a bit of dirt ever do anybody any harm?' By mid-morning it was too hot even to face the walk down to the river to swim, given the return trudge through the fields carrying Callum. In her

fifth week Lynn said, 'Although I enjoy teaching the children and playing with them, I can't do it for the next five weeks. It's just not me.'

                                                 ℬ ℭ

One Monday morning towards the end February *make* Shongwe said to Lynn, 'There has been a death in the family. We have just heard that one of my husband's sisters has died.' The sister was twenty-six-year-old Ntombifuthi, daughter of *umkhulu*'s elder brother Mcasane. The message had come from her mother, who had never married Mcasane. Ntombifuthi had died quite suddenly after a short illness involving abdominal cramps. Her body was already at the undertaker's. *Babe* Shongwe, as Mcasane's oldest son and heir, would have to bury her.

The British shrink from death. Robert's reaction was typical. Once he heard that the body would lie in an open coffin in the Great Hut, he decided to take the children and run, for a day or two. He said resentfully, 'Just as they are getting used to this way of life, this happens. They've taken seven weeks to adjust. I don't want to mess them up. Chloe is already asking all sorts of questions. I know exactly how they tick. This is something that is going to frighten them.' He need not have been so defensive. Swazis too keep their children away from death, though for different reasons. They think the spirit of a newly deceased person is dangerous and unpredictable until it has been ceremonially called back to the homestead. Children are too vulnerable to be exposed at this perilous time.

Robert had never seen a corpse. He hated going to funerals and felt no obligation to go

Home school: while the children worked at their assignments, Lynn read.

to this one. 'I didn't even meet the woman. Her death hasn't touched me personally. I'm not gonna be there. It'll give my children nightmares for fifteen years. I wanted them to experience Africa, but this is one of the things I don't want them to experience at their age.'

Unlike most British people, Lynn, as a nurse, had seen death often. In the hospital she had often helped people who were dying. She observed, 'At home people get upset and distraught because death is so unusual. Here death happens every day. It's all around you. There's not usually a nice undertaker. You have to take an active part. I don't think it's a bad thing. If you meet death head-on it's less frightening.' Nonetheless she was torn between going with the children to a hotel for a night, and staying on the homestead to do what she could. She said, 'I'm an outsider. I live here, but I'm not really part of it. I don't know the girl who died or the people who are coming to stay. I'll stay if *make* Shongwe really wants me to.'

Make Shongwe really did want her to. Lynn was really part of it. To Robert's great surprise, he found he was part of it too. Later that day, sitting with the other men in the Great Hut discussing the burial, he heard himself accepting the assumption that he would be one of the men of the homestead who went up the slopes of the mountain to dig the grave at midnight. He had not realized how the funeral was affecting the homestead. He came out of the Great Hut chastened. 'Even though they're not my blood relatives, I've lived with them very, very closely these last seven weeks. Since I've been here the whole African experience hasn't been real to me, but this funeral is real. Someone dying isn't a joke. I'm going to give them all the support I can.'

At first Lynn and Robert were indignant that Ntombifuthi's burial should be *babe*

Shongwe's responsibility. Robert said, 'She didn't ever come here. She isn't part of the community. When was the last time they saw this woman?' It was true that nobody had seen Ntombifuthi for some years. Her half-sisters, arriving for the funeral, tried to remember what she looked like. Everybody knew she had two children by different fathers, and that they had been given to their fathers' families. Robert thought this settled the matter of funeral costs. 'I'd go to these two useless men and say, "Look, your missus is dead. Each of you's got kids with her, so what are you going to contribute?"'

Mandla also argued that the two fathers owed them something. Neither father had compensated the family for impregnating his sister. 'Let's go and ask them for *inhlawulo*, damages,' he suggested. It was not a practical suggestion. Such negotiations take years.

Lynn thought the Shongwes should ask all the relatives for a donation. That was what people in Britain would do if they were hard up and somebody had died. *Make* Shongwe was appalled. Lynn thought the rest of the relatives were taking advantage of *babe* Shongwe. 'Everybody is sucking *babe* Shongwe dry. This really isn't the extended family at all.' But it was the extended family at its best. Afterwards Lynn was able to concede that. The Shongwes were in no doubt that the responsibility for the funeral was theirs. Ntombifuthi was the unmarried child of the late homestead head. She must be brought home.

Lynn went with them to the undertaker and watched them resist the high-pressure sales pitch. Ntombifuthi should have had funeral insurance, the salesman told them. Every person on the street could afford five pounds a month for funeral insurance. With proper insurance, Ntombifuthi would have been entitled to a coffin costing £500, with £500 over to feed the mourners. That, he said, would have put her into the middle-income class of coffin. High-income people paid more than £1,000 – even £2,000. Unashamed by all this, the Shongwes sensibly settled for one of the very cheapest coffins. They knew their true worth. It was catch-22. If they hired a pick-up privately, they would have to pay mortuary fees to the undertaker and a cow to the pick-up owner, to purge his vehicle from the contamination of death.

Lynn felt awkward, an intruder at the mortuary. 'I thought it was a matter for proper family, not people like me, pretending to be family.' But she was wrong. The more she behaved like proper family, the more they appreciated it. She said, 'I can't feel upset', but the funeral was not about feeling, it was about doing. Lynn and Robert did magnificently.

Robert woke after midnight and went in the darkness to the family burial place at the foot of the mountain to help the men dig the grave. The Shongwes loved him for it. One of *babe* Shongwe's sisters said, 'If Ntombifuthi were to wake up and see English people digging her grave, she'd be tickled pink!'

After the burial, when the men were sitting around finishing their meal, *umkhulu* summarized her brief life history, which was rich with the complexity of Swazi family customs. His brother had never married Ntombifuthi's mother, but he took responsibility for the child. When she was still very young she had been given as a subordinate co-wife, *inhlanti*, to her *anti*, her father's married sister. This common custom allows a man to acquire a second wife from the family who gave him his first wife, without the necessity to pay any more *lobolo*. Unhappily, both her aunt and her husband died before

Ntombifuthi had borne any children, but one of their sons, who was there at the funeral, remembered her as one of his mothers, although he was actually older than she was.

Lynn sat up half the night in the great tent that had been erected to extend the Great Hut, and sang and prayed and clapped with the other women. She kept her knees on the ground and her legs straight until her bones ached. She wore her apron and covered her head. She accompanied Ntombifuthi's body to the graveside. Everybody admired her pinny and headscarf. They had expressed surprise at her fulsome participation. She helped to serve people food from the tables that the Shongwes had constructed in impromptu fashion by balancing sheets of corrugated iron on empty oil drums. She took away people's empty plates. The more they admired, the more she tried to do what the Shongwes wanted her to do. The Shongwes, visitors and homestead alike, were all impressed. *Make* Shongwe remarked, 'She's really changed. She worked so hard.' And then, the ultimate compliment, 'It's time we paid her *lobolo*.' Lynn had passed her probation; she was worth paying for.

Lynn felt useful and accepted for the first time. She said, 'All in all, it's been a good funeral. It has helped me to feel part of what's going on. I've been a good Swazi housewife. I haven't offended anyone. People have been really nice to me.' She acknowledged that she had not always tried hard enough to oblige the Shongwes. She had been 'a bit rebellious. I haven't done everything I could to fit in completely.' Instead, she had been 'carrying on in my own little way in private. I don't know if it upset them.' Of course it had. Lynn's notion of smoking 'in private' was to lie on her bed with the door ajar. Baring her legs in private meant untying her long skirt before she reached the road. Sitting improperly in private meant with her legs cocked at the bus stop.

Her rebellion had not been without principle. That principle was a very Western one: 'I want to be accepted for what I am.' Steadily she had resisted the rules. She still wore her apron, but only when she wanted to. 'I'll put it on for anything dirty, not because anybody wants me to, but because it's practical.' Her use of the headscarf was likewise getting 'a bit lax'. She reduced it to a narrow cloth headband, and did not always wear even that. 'I'm not traipsing around the homestead with a pinny on, any more than I'm traipsing around with a headscarf on!' She said, 'It's now easier to say, "I want to do this, I want to do that", without worrying what they're going to think about me. If I don't want to do something, I won't do it.' She no longer did the bidding of the men of the homestead just because they were men. When Mandla asked her impatiently for more food, she said, 'Mandla! I have one pair of hands and they are actually occupied already. Could you stop being so impatient.' Curiously, the one rule she felt constrained to keep, even in private, was the avoidance of homestead eggs. She put it down to residual guilt about breaking all the other rules.

Now she felt she had triumphed. 'There are things about them I'll never agree with, and there are things about me they'll never agree with. We've reached a stage of understanding and mutual respect.' Now she was willing to 'damp my Western bit down a bit'. She realized that it was important to the Shongwes that she behaved in a certain manner. As for being a daughter-in-law, she said, 'They don't think I'm a daughter-in-law for a moment. I'm more an honoured guest. And a source of amusement.'

Lynn and make *Shongwe share a domestic moment at the tap.*

CHAPTER FIFTEEN
'dodging the last hurdle'

While Robert was looking for work he came back with tales of people he had seen, places he had been to, things he had eaten. Lynn was resentful. He was less and less her New Man. He was backsliding, and the Swazis were aiding and abetting him with their rules about men's work and women's work. Men did all the exciting things; even when they were at home they were constantly off the homestead, looking for cattle on top of the mountain, going down to the cattle dip, consulting the chief at the other end of the neighbourhood. And when they returned, she said, they were treated like little princes. They sank on to the nearest upturned bucket and, in a trice, some woman was kneeling before them, with a tub of something slightly alcoholic to drink, assuring them that there was food if they were hungry. They never lifted a finger to feed themselves. They were waited on hand and foot. Lynn did not want Robert to conform to this stereotype and she said so, stridently, both to him and to them.

The Shongwe women listened to her criticisms politely. They watched Robert washing the children's dishes, warming water and carrying it to the house. They talked among themselves. *Gogo* laKhanyile said, 'Doing everything for a man isn't slavery. It's respect. We are below men in the hierarchy. That man' – she indicated Robert – 'he cooks! He wipes his child's bottom! Their country is bad!' She outlined her views on the proper division of

(opposite)
Robert flouts local custom by insisting that he, rather than his children, share the domestic work with Lynn.

The Western world is never far away from the homestead. Swaziland has had its own daily newspaper for over a century.

labour between a married couple. Significantly, she referred to the woman not as the man's wife, but as the man's parents' daughter-in-law; Swazi marriage is more about a woman coming to join a homestead than it is about a couple settling down together. That is why women have to be taught the rules, not left to invent them, as the Nestors did when they married. *Gogo* explained, 'As a daughter-in-law I must respect my husband. I came to him; it's his right as a man. If he constructs the walls of the house, I do the roof. If he farms, I weed. As for cooking, it's for women. Cleaning children is also for women. The husband's duty is to check the cattle. Washing my husband's clothes is a sign of love. If a husband did your washing, you'd think he'd been bewitched. Cultures differ, but I don't envy their culture.'

It is the obligation of the homestead head to ensure that people keep these rules. When a wife fails in her duty, her husband takes up the matter not with her, but with his father. *Make* Shongwe said, 'When I am naughty I have to come to the Great Hut. When I upset *babe* Shongwe, he has to tell *umkhulu*. *Umkhulu* has to call me to the Great Hut. We have to sit down and sort it out. I have to apologize, "Sorry, *umkhulu*, I did not know that was wrong.' A wife's apology is due, not to her husband but to the whole family, represented by the homestead head.

Lynn listened and declared that she had no intention of behaving towards Robert as a Swazi wife would. Contrary to the Swazi arrangement, she set her own ideal of the complete elimination of all gender distinctions. 'There's no such thing as women's work,' she argued.

'That's not the Swazi way,' *make* Shongwe replied. Lynn returned to argue this theme with *make* Shongwe time and again, but never as shrilly as when, in their seventh week, intensely bored with the narrow domestic life she had created for herself on the homestead, she went to inform *make* Shongwe that she and Robert had agreed to swap roles. She would go and look for a job and earn some cash; he would stay at home with the children and do the tasks daughters-in-law did.

The Shongwes, tolerant of many of the ways of these strangers in their midst, put their foot down when they heard about Lynn's plan for Robert to take on the role of a daughter-in-law. She could go and find paid work if she wished. Plenty of women did so. But Lynn could not expect the other women of the homestead to accept Robert as a co-worker in their women's tasks. 'It's not the right way. If you are a wife, you wake up early and do your home work before you leave, or you hire somebody to look after your job at the homestead,' *make* Shongwe explained. The allocation of work on the homestead had nothing to do with whether or not they were in paid employment. *Umkhulu* would not stand for it. It was a serious issue that would have to be discussed at the Great Hut. Lynn, in campaigning mode, received this statement with a laugh and departed to look for work, shouting over her shoulder that none of the women of the homestead were under any circumstances to do Robert's work for him.

Lynn viewed the matter of who did what as a private issue to be resolved by a couple who, between them, had no option but to get all of their household's work done. The homestead is a quite different social unit. It has a much bigger pool of labour, which it uses economically. There are, as Lynn had often ruefully observed, lots of children, for a start. Once children have shouldered their share of the work, what is left for the adults is less onerous. The rules are not negotiated. They are laid down by cultural consensus.

As in almost all African societies, women are important – sometimes the main, agricultural labourers. This is the logical counterpart of women's responsibility to provide the meals. Hoes are women's tools. Men get involved in agriculture whenever oxen or tractors are used, for cattle are always the men's responsibility and tractors come from the West where men, rather than women, are the farmers and the mechanics. Childcare tends to be left to the other children. When, by demographic accident, there are no children, then children will be borrowed and lent, to fill the gap. Lynn encountered such an arrangement when she went health visiting with *gogo* laNkhosi. Two ageing widowed co-wives were being cared for by the daughter of the woman they had been given, and had brought up, as their own child, two generations earlier.

Off the homestead all these rules dissolve. Migrant workers have to adapt to new circumstances. In the single men's quarters, such as *umkhulu* has been allocated, or the shared room such as *babe* Shongwe occupies, men cook, clean and wash their own clothes just like the single men they have temporarily become. They have learnt all these domestic skills as boys on the homestead. Many find girl-friends to help them in these tiresome tasks, or arrange for an adolescent child to be sent to live with them and help out.

Lynn's demand that – in the interests of settling a score in the sex war that she was conducting with her husband – she be allowed to disrupt the homestead's system of the division of labour by age, sex and marital status struck the Shongwes as impertinence. *Make* Shongwe said, 'It's not for *make* Nestor to say that *babe* Nestor is looking after the children. That's not the way the homestead is living here. This is a Swazi homestead. We need *babe* Nestor to harvest the maize. If *umkhulu* can find a man sitting in the kitchen, he is going to say, "No way! Men are not doing that!" A man's job is to sit outside the men's enclosure, looking after the *kraal*, looking at what is going on outside, not sitting in the kitchen.'

Thus, to her chagrin, when Lynn went to work, Robert was spared all the domestic duties she so badly wanted him to experience. Thandi laMabuza scrubbed and polished their floor, and washed their clothes, much as she had been doing ever since Lynn's princi-pled rejection of Xolile's help. Robert sat around the homestead for a day or two, enter-taining the children. Then, bored with inac-tivity, he went to see Dokta and proposed that the time had come for them to try their hand at setting up a roadside stall.

৯ ৫

The work that Lynn had found without much trouble was as a nursing assistant in Manzini's only hospital, founded by American mission-aries and now funded mainly by the govern-ment. The out-patient department still comes to a halt for fifteen minutes every morning while prayers are prayed and hymns are sung. Swazi patients do not seem to mind. It is part of the deal and they sing along.

Lynn was attached to the maternity ward, where her job was to help to bath the newborn babies. They deliver more than fifty babies a day, so there was a lot of bathing. The mothers, who stay in the hospital for as little as twelve hours, watched through a glass screen as their babies were unwrapped, cried, were soaped and then dunked in clean warm water. They bobbed politely to Lynn as they received their clean, wrapped babies back. It was a strictly functional business. Lynn compared unfavourably the perfunctory way in which the bathing was being done with the indulgent routines of bathing new babies in Britain, but the comparison was unfair; nurses are not mothers. 'This is the school of hard knocks,' she said. 'It starts with your first bath. It starts rough and it gets rougher.'

She was struck by what she described as the subdued atmosphere in the maternity ward. 'Nobody seems overly pleased with their babies. There are no cards, no presents, no flowers. I'm not saying it's right or wrong,' she added, 'there's just less fuss here,' She rightly saw that births in places with a very high birth rate are less special. Although the Swazi birth rate has been falling quite steeply, each woman still has on average just under six children. One might also expect less celebra-tion in a place with a high infant death rate. International agencies frown on Swaziland's infant death rate, but in 1998 only one in a hundred infants died in the first year of life. This rate is likely to escalate. One-third of all women giving birth in Swaziland are now HIV-positive; 10 per cent of all babies are born HIV-positive, while another 20 per cent

are likely to become infected as they suckle. All of these are likely
to die before they reach school age. The social impact of these
statistics is only just beginning to be felt.

But the subdued atmosphere in the maternity ward is not due
to depression about reduced longevity. It is, as the Swazis say,
cultural. Fathers are not meant to see their newborn babies for
weeks, even months. Among royals the rule is six months. Women
are meant to be 'confined' – put away – after giving birth. The
higher your status, the more you are confined. Those giving birth
at home remain alone in a hut; only the more affluent can afford
a long period of this kind of confinement, but everybody attempts
a decent period of isolation. Babies remain covered for their own
protection; until they have been introduced to their ancestors
they are vulnerable to all sorts of malign forces. Mothers are
anxious not to draw attention to them. As for receiving cards and
flowers, these lie right outside the cultural repertoire. The giving
of flowers when a child is born is, in its absolute uselessness, a
European custom that Swazis despise.

*Lynn as nurse. She is
attending one of* umkhulu's
wives, gogo *laNkhosi, the
rural health motivator,
who was unwell.*

Most rural Swazi children are breastfed on demand for at least a year.

(opposite)
Make *Shongwe baths her smallest children every morning before pre-school. By the age of six Swazi children bath themselves.*

Lynn felt very comfortable being back in a hospital. After seven weeks on the unfamiliar homestead, she was back in a familiar and predictable environment. 'I just walk into a ward and feel at home. It's all second nature.' She found the nurses easy to talk to. 'I was chatting away within a couple of seconds. In the homestead it took four to five weeks to realize what I had in common.' The Swazi nurses' training had been almost the same as hers. They instantly found common ground. They moaned about salaries and matrons. They looked at Tupperware catalogues together. Lynn said, 'I can now have a laugh with *make* Shongwe and *make* laMabuza, but not on the same level as I've done within forty-eight hours here.'

Working as a nursing assistant, her days on the ward were without stress. When the babies had all been bathed, she made up the beds, with one sheet and some prickly grey cotton blankets. She sponged down soiled mattresses.

She was spared the more gruelling chores of the nursing assistant, because in Swaziland patients are expected to do more for themselves. 'They clean up their own blood, vomit, urine.' Their relatives, rather than the nursing staff, are their carers. But Lynn was struck by the similarities rather than the differences between hospitals in Britain and Swaziland. 'The hospitals at home that haven't been refurbished are exactly like this.'

She found the hospital routines strikingly similar. She thought the differences lay in patients' expectations. Patients sometimes had to sleep on the floor under other

patients' beds. Lynn thought that was just the result of a different attitude to admissions. In Britain, where they worry more about controlling infection, they turn people away rather than push the beds closer together. In Swaziland everybody who needs hospitalization is admitted; they just squeeze them in. To her surprise, a great many of the nurses were Swazi men. She had once again underestimated the importance of situation; just as men living alone do all the things proscribed for men living with wives, so men in work will, when the job requires it, do tasks they would otherwise leave for women.

There was something else contributing to her sense of contentment; the hospital job came with the use of a furnished house. It had electricity, television, a bath and hot running water. But, better than all this, it was on a main road. She loved the hustle and bustle. She could sit on the verandah and listen to the roar of the traffic. She could watch people walking past. She commented, 'Don't get me wrong. It's nice sitting on the homestead chatting, when the sky is really clear, and with the crickets and stuff, but I prefer to sit on the verandah watching people walk past. It's more normal. I could be anywhere in the world. Here I feel less lonely by myself than I do on the homestead surrounded by people.' She soaked in a hot bath. She lay in bed and listened to the traffic and found it far less disturbing than the Shongwes' rooster.

Robert and the children came to visit, and they stayed. They watched pop stars singing familiar songs on television, they showered, they cooked their food on a fire and called it a barbecue. Robert said of the house, 'It's not exactly a palace, is it?' but nonetheless he worried a bit about being there. Was he cheating? It was not rural

Swaziland. On the other hand, it was the kind of place in which a Swazi from a rural homestead might well live during the week, if he happened to get work as a hospital administrator. He said, 'I can't quite put my finger on it. We only have a few days left in the country. In some way we've dodged the last hurdle.'

Robert's confusion was understandable. The boundaries between rural and urban life are entirely porous in Swaziland. Since almost everybody belongs to a rural homestead, it follows that even people living in gracious bungalows with swimming pools have another place, in some chiefdom, where their parents live, where their cattle graze, where they go at weekends, where their children spend part of their lives. Living in town is a common element of the rural homestead experience.

What Robert had dodged was a week of being 'stuck' (as Lynn phrased it) on the homestead with the children. He had dodged the role-reversal that Lynn had challenged him to accept – the women of the homestead saw to that. So, finding himself with no domestic chores except entertaining his children, he had done the good Swazi thing; he had finally tried to make money by selling something.

This idea had been simmering as a possibility for the Nestors from their very first weeks on the homestead. The roads of Swaziland are littered with the skeletons of failed roadside stalls: hastily erected wooden structures, built with more optimism than market research. Robert favoured a semi-derelict row near the entrance to the university, where some successful traders had established themselves selling canned drinks, grilled chickens and rice to students. He took the children with him to scout out the possibilities. He discovered that trading-licence

inspections were rare and that nobody seemed to lay claim to the derelict stalls. Together with Dokta, he selected a sturdy one ankle-deep in grass. All they needed, he said confidently, was capital for the foodstuffs, transport and the use of some basic cooking equipment.

He talked to *make* Shongwe, who liked the idea. 'Rather than look for jobs, it's better to employ yourself.' The homestead needed a stall where it could sell its produce. It was, she said, a perfect opportunity for Dokta on his free days and her ne'er-do-well brother Makhosini had a pick-up. She would love to see him working, instead of loafing around impregnating women. Maybe she would sell items there herself, with Thandeka on her back. She agreed to invest five pounds in the stall. Robert, who the previous day had talked about having twenty-five pounds to invest, rapidly reduced his available capital to five pounds to match hers. Dokta said that, by borrowing, he could probably raise another four pounds and a paraffin stove to cook on. *Make* Shongwe lent them two empty drums as tables, some saucepans and a worn tarpaulin in case of rain. She also gave them four loaves of bread.

Robert's plan – if plan is the right word – was to sell hotdogs to students. He had found a shop in town that sold tinned frank-furters. All they needed now was a supply of bread rolls and some

Makeshift stalls are a common sight along Swazi roads. Running one proved more difficult than Robert expected.

hot fried onions. 'We can't expect to make a profit at the beginning,' he said, enigmatically. 'It'll take a week or two, maybe three, to break even.' Nobody challenged his economics. In a week or two he would be well out of it, driving his lorry around London.

The hotdog stall was not a success. On the first day they spent about nine pounds buying bread rolls, matches, cooking oil, synthetic drink concentrate, polystyrene cups and paper towels, and had taken less than two pounds before the rain came down in torrents. The tarpaulin leaked and flapped in the wind. They all got soaked and went home.

On the second day, still dithering about the price they should charge, they shouted their wares, like London market-traders, to the amazement of the students, who all steered clear of them. Robert advised, 'Open another can of sausages! Fry some onions! When the customers smell the food cooking they will come.' They did not. Then Robert tried the hard sell. He went on to the campus and waylaid students. 'Taste the orange juice! What do you think of it? You get it free with a hotdog for three *emalangeni* fifty. Tell me if that ain't cheap!'

Daniel squirmed with embarrassment. 'My God! He's mental!' He cornered students approaching the chicken stall. 'You gonna buy some manky old chicken and rice when I'm selling you hotdogs?' They were indeed.

By the end of the second day they had served six customers. Robert said, 'It'll take a day or two', and shared out the remaining hotdogs among his family. Makhosini and Dokta dipped leftover bread into the hot water in which the sausages had been warmed.

'The business is theirs,' said Makhosini, who had not been paid for his petrol. 'Daniel said we could not have a hotdog. This juice is

soup from the hotdogs. It tastes nice. It's OK. We've been hungry.'

Robert explained, 'It hasn't quite worked yet.' Then he added optimistically, 'I didn't expect to make loads of money in the first week.'

They considered what they might be doing wrong. Makhosini thought their approach was too crude for the student market. 'This is an institute of higher learning. They don't like something that has been cooked by paraffin.'

Dokta agreed. 'The paraffin puts people off. I hear customers talking about the paraffin.' What they needed was a portable gas cooker, tomato sauce and margarine to spread on the rolls.

Makhosini thought the hard sales pitch was all wrong. 'We should try to improve the way we communicate with them. We should socialize, try to be friendly with them.' He also thought Daniel should stop serving onions with a knife. He explained, 'It's against our custom. Food served with a knife will cause trouble.'

On the third day Daniel offered his opinion on Robert's partners. 'When the customers come, they're not quick off the mark. They're nice as people, but they're not very good business people. Half the stock's gone missing, eaten by whatever-his-name-is. I think the stall will stop when we go. My dad goes out and pesters till people buy. They just sit and wait. It's just the Swazi way, I think. After three weeks they'll pack up.'

By the end of the week Robert was ready to withdraw. 'I showed them what to do. It's not complicated. Daniel can do it and he's only thirteen. It's down to them. To stay here another week will be a week too long for me.' He said to Makhosini, 'I'll see you on Monday at eight', but he never went back to the stall. Something had happened to deeply disillusion him about Dokta. Robert wanted nothing more to do with him.

What Dokta had done was what Dokta often did. He had gone off on a drinking spree. It was the kind of thing Robert himself might do, but there was a difference: Dokta had left his wife and children without either food or money. LaSibandze had come knocking on Robert's door. Robert said, 'Nobody's ever asked me for food before. Nobody's ever knocked on my door and said, "I'm hungry." It's a weird feeling.' He was shocked. 'She's a proud woman. He put her in that situation, where she had to stoop to that sort of level, to ask for food. I didn't like it that she had to do that. He had enough money to buy his missus mealie meal, but he chose not to do so.'

It was a recurrent crisis of a kind not uncommon among Swazis, and the options for coping with it were already in place. Despite *make* Shongwe's urging that she stay and discuss the matter once more at the Great Hut, Dokta's wife and their youngest child returned to her father's homestead, blaming the Shongwe homestead for her predicament. She had been willing to go and work on the pineapple plantations, but they had mocked her, saying how could she wear overalls and live in the urban slum with plantation workers. The only work they had been willing to approve for her was selling vegetables with *gogo* laNkhosi, which she had no intention of doing. She was going back home. Marriages among Swazis are not particularly stable, but there is generally little fall-out. Dokta's three oldest children simply moved in with *babe* Shongwe. The Nestors saw this as further exploitation of Themba's largesse and goodwill, but it was not that at all. It was a case

of the descent-based homestead exercising its time-tested principles of responsibility and obligation. It was not for nothing that Dokta's children call Themba their 'big father'.

Dokta was there on the Nestors' last day at the homestead, dressed in his traditional best. An integral part of the Shongwe homestead, despite his misdemeanours, he carried lightly, as his inalienable right, his passing dependence on his brothers and fathers. Robert avoided catching Dokta's eye, but it was otherwise an unemotional farewell. Only Lynn thought of weeping. The Nestors, forgetting the elasticity of homestead membership, got into a bit of a muddle trying to give everyone a farewell gift. They gave away many of their clothes, and Daniel, Chloe and Callum recirculated their least-loved books and toys.

They all piled into the Great Hut for final prayers, songs and speeches. Chloe sang with the girls like a Swazi. *Umkhulu* said he hoped the Nestors would return, but if not them, then perhaps some other British people. *Babe* Shongwe thanked the Nestors for their support during Ntombifuthi's funeral and then reminded them that they had spoken of finding investors overseas who would help them obtain electricity. Robert thanked the Shongwes for treating them like part of the family. He said, 'You'll always be part of my life.'

Afterwards he commented, 'I'm not good at goodbyes. I didn't want to get attached to the situation. That's what scared me the last two weeks. We'd started breaking down barriers. I wanted to get it over and done with, and get out as quickly as I could. Nice and quick. Just go.'

The Nestors piled into the waiting pickup and went.

EPILOGUE

When Lynn got back to her house in London at the end of March, she said, 'It's like I've never been away.' She was unpacking her tourist trophies in front of her welcoming friends, who had spring-cleaned the house for her and brought her flowers. She had been doing what she called 'a huge amount of retail therapy' in the week since she had left the homestead. Out came her Swazi apron and headscarf. She put them on and pirouetted, saying, 'I used to wear my hair up. I looked hideous. This looked particularly fetching with gumboots. I was the real *make*, I'm telling you! *Make* Nestor.' As Robert looked in on the scene – women, children, opened suitcases, possessions everywhere – she asked him, 'Does this bring back memories, darling?' Swaziland was becoming a distant memory, distorted – as all memories are. Had she ever been a real *make*?

There had been moments, at the beginning when she had tried to be, when her contraventions of the homestead rules had been surreptitious, when her incompetence at women's domestic duties had humiliated her. But they had been shortlived when she realised that in many ways they were being treated as honoured guests by the Shongwes. But there were limits that even honoured guests had to respect. To the Nestors' surprise, they were expected to inform the homestead of their plans whenever they went away. Their first infringement of this rule, during their first week, had brought a swift reprimand in the Great Hut. *Umhkulu* tells the story: 'They said they were going to the river for a shower. We started wondering what happened to them, since it started getting darker. We were worried that they might be attacked by animals in the river. We feared that if these people got injured or disappeared, we would be liable because they were under our custody. Later we received information that a taxi had collected them along the way to the dip-tank and taken them to Manzini. We do not like such things, because one day we might receive reports that they were found dead in a place we do not even know.'

The Nestors found themselves obliged to respect the rules that the homestead laid down for the work done by Swazi children. But the strongest resistance from the homestead came when Lynn attempted to get Robert to do the work of a homestead woman. This was beyond the pale, even for an honoured guest. Lynn's passionate demand that Robert should be permitted this experience was beyond the Shongwes' understanding. When *make* Shongwe said, 'Never!', Lynn replied, 'Never say *never*! Things can change!' and urged *make* Shongwe to come to England and see. If the Shongwes were to conduct the same social experiment as the Nestors, then a meeting of minds on some of the inevitable cultural clashes might be more likely.

Make Shongwe's reply was subtle, 'One day, one day, but just for one day.'

Lynn had come to Africa expecting Robert to be tremendously occupied in men's tasks, while she happily did women's work, but Westerners can easily misunderstand both the nature and the scope of men's and women's work. Much of Swazi men's work in the homestead is managerial, advisory and administrative. This remained invisible to the Nestors. The Nestors never saw *umkhulu* at the chief's seat, sorting out the week-by-week issues of the community. They never heard the informal talk in the Great Hut as he received visits from neighbours and reiterated principles for the resolution of conflicts. Robert never participated in negotiations for the return of Mandla's children, or for the damages due following the impregnation of three daughters of the homestead. It is men's work to maintain the warp of this social fabric as it stretches across clans, and it is a demanding task from which Robert, with no knowledge of SiSwati, was inevitably excluded.

The Nestors saw the Shongwe men only during their relatively leisured moments at home – ploughing, digging, weeding, tending cattle, repairing buildings, sitting, talking, planning – when they were not at their paid work. Both Robert and Lynn thought them tremendously idle compared to the women, with their more visible home-based tasks. Yet even the women they considered idle, compared to the Swazi children. On the other hand, when Lynn saw women doing non-domestic work she thought it 'very, very scary' that women were being 'pushed further and further into a man's world while still chained to a kitchen sink'.

The Nestors gained a limited, seasonal view of Swazi community life during their short visit. They saw the cooking, the clean-ing, the childcare, but not *gogo* laNkhosi's days selling at the market; they saw Thandi laMabuza's piles of grass in the shed, but not her long winter hours of labour up on the mountain, cutting it; they saw the tins of mealie meal in the kitchen, but not the long, hot walks to and from the mill carrying the grain. They saw *make* Shongwe sitting on her kitchen steps, excusing herself from tasks that younger people could do and arguing, tongue in cheek, that she was 'just a pretty face', but not her years as an employee in the handicraft industry supporting her mother and children with essential cash. In ten short weeks, they could not see the homestead's past, nor its future.

ಬಿ ಛ

Lynn wanted to change Swaziland almost as soon as she arrived. The way they differenti-ated men from women, boys from girls, was only part of it. She wanted to make the coun-try more efficient, more like Britain. She found the Swazis distressingly complacent, too satisfied with things as they were. As she said in week one, 'There doesn't seem to be

any will to change. It seems to be cast in stone. All people say is, "That's the way it is."'

She did not like the time everything took. It took time to walk to the bus; the buses did not run to schedule, so it took more time waiting for them. The people in shops served you slowly, and you had to queue for hours to pay the school fees. 'Everybody accepts these situations without so much as a shrug of the shoulders. For me it's not sensible. There has to be a better way.' She could not accept what she described as 'this laid-back, "yeah, it's there, so we'll accept it" sort of attitude'. She became a crusader for change, fighting by example. From the very first week she modi-fied her original intention to fit in as much as she could, she said instead, 'I'll be living my version of a Swazi life.'

Robert had wanted to go to Africa because he was black. His expectations were high and his sympathies strong. His first impressions were very positive: he wanted to blend in, he wanted to belong. He was dismayed by Lynn's initial inability to cope with the homestead's customs, but never once attributed it to her race; nor did she, except for the moment when Xolile was given to her, when she felt that 'as a white' she could not accept this gift. Most of the time Lynn does not feel white at all; she says, 'My children are mixed; they're part of me. My family are ancestors of black people to come.' Both Robert and Lynn found the Swazis to be with-out a trace of racism. Robert said, 'Nobody's got them sort of vibes here.'

Yet inevitably there were elements of the African experience that, right from the start, Robert found alien. Unlike Lynn he tolerated the way Swazis discriminated on the basis of sex: he found it interesting and comfortable to be in a society in which a clear distinction was drawn between the roles and responsibilities of men and women, with men formally having the upper hand. After a week on the homestead he said, 'We men get up and do what we want to do. It's not a problem for me, but it is for Lynn. I don't agree with it, but they're not my rules. I've got to live the way they live. There is a sort of a balance here and you can't just come in from the outside and dictate to people. They've got their rules, which they've had for God-knows-how-many years, so I'm not going to interfere.' He thought the restrictions to which Lynn, as a daughter-in-law, was subjected were 'not fair by our standards, but by their standards they are fair'. As a temporary experience, they had to be tolerated although 'If she was living here for good I'd say, "No she can't walk around in temperatures of ninety degrees covering her head and everything else."'

Five weeks later he felt that his family was adapting well to the new and different expectations that the homestead had of them. Lynn was buckling down to domestic work, and the children were learning to 'muck in and help out, and they didn't want to do it, because that's not what they do at home'. As for himself, he conceded, 'It's been very, very easy for me, being basically bone idle; doing nothing and waiting for my meals. Waiting for a woman to crash down on her knees and say, "Here's a meal, sir."'

He tolerated less successfully the need to be subservient in the Swazi workplace. 'Living here is not easy. You have to bite your tongue and humble yourself. The only thing that makes it easy for me is that it's not for good.' He is a proud person, his British culture has taught him that subservience is unnecessary and, as a black British man, he is particularly sensitive about inferiority. He found being a

waiter demeaning, especially when most of the guests were white and most of those serving them black. But he managed it. 'I'd only do this for a week. This sort of environment is not for me.'

Corporal punishment of children at school was another testing issue. Robert withdrew Daniel from school, rather than let him be subject to the threat of a caning. There was both a personal and a philosophical objection to controlling children through fear and force. The Nestors argued against the Swazi practice of hitting their children.

The Swazi supernatural beliefs that he encountered were beyond anything Robert, like most Westerners, had previously experienced. First there was the Jericho church, with its colourful and animated spirit possessions, which he regarded as 'too primitive' and probably bogus. 'If the people who actually go to the church every Sunday can't explain it, how can I explain it? If I'm going to any sort of ceremony I've got to know what it's about.' Even less comprehensible in Western terms was his visit to the traditional healer to solve Dokta's unemployment problem. To Robert, as a British person, the Swazi assumption that unemployment might be due to ancestral anger or witchcraft seemed irrational, and the visit to the healer emphasized the fact that Robert did not belong. It made him feel British.

Outside the *sangoma*'s hut Robert said, 'I always wanted to go to Africa. But there's only one place you can call home. It's where you were born: London. This is Africa, but it's not where I was born. I feel like a foreigner. I feel like a total outsider. When you get down to it, who can I relate to while I'm here? No one. Themba and Mandla and Dokta treat me like a brother, but at the dead of night, when we're all talking, I can't join in. I'm not talking siSwati. Nobody on the homestead would understand London. London is another world. I'm a visitor here. The only link is the fact that we're black.' He added wistfully, 'It would have been good to find the spirit of Africa here, but I didn't.'

What Robert liked about Swaziland, was the warm community spirit of the homestead. But that, he thought, had nothing to do with colour, or with being African; it was simply about being human. He contrasted it with the anonymity and indifference of people in his London neighbourhood. After twelve years in the same house he was only just beginning to know his London neighbours. 'We ain't got no time for anyone. Everybody's always rushing around. I'm the same. It's a two-way thing. Here I slow right down.' He speculated on the chilly reception that a Swazi family might receive in a London neighbourhood. 'They wouldn't be treated the way we've been treated here.'

He hoped the children would remember how kind people on the homestead had been. 'It was like we'd been away for a long, long time and we were coming home.' But he recognized that the lifestyle went with the place. 'You can't transfer this lifestyle to London.' Back in London he would 'snap back into the groove: money, bills, clothes'. 'Like a rat in a wheel chasing my tail.' It was his fate. But he could never live long-term on a homestead. 'I've seen how they have to struggle. They're born here, bred here, but it's no free ride.'

When Robert first arrived at the homestead he saw only material deprivation and kindness. In his first week he said, 'I think they're really resourceful. Everything they use is from the earth. Even the rope is made from grass. I respect that. They're survivors. They haven't got flash cars, but what they've got they use. They might not be surviving on the level we have, but their kids are fed. I've never seen any of their kids starving. They grow their food and they eat it. There's never anything spare for them to sell, but they're surviving till something better comes along. It's a very peaceful community.' But the longer the Nestors stayed on the homestead, the more they realized they were simply skimming the surface of a very complex institution. Robert said, 'On the surface, the homestead looks very simple. Underneath it's a complex little community. The way they have to interact and try to solve each other's problems is complicated.' He said, 'I've been gliding around like a tourist. It's not as easy and straightforward as it looks.' They began to see malevolence and potential wealth. The began to speculate on how the homestead could *progress*.

By international standards, Swazis are not poor. The World Bank ranks Swaziland as a middle-income country. Some of this income goes to the few large investors (the king among them), but Swazi society is structured to ensure a remarkably equitable distribution among the rest. The homestead, with its porous boundaries, is at the centre of the system of income redistribution. Just ten weeks on the Shongwe homestead demonstrated this clearly to the Nestors and they did not always like it. *Babe* Shongwe's wages were stretched to cover not only his own children's school fees, but those of his unemployed brother; *gogo* laKhanyile's grain store was opened to feed her sister's grandchildren living fifty miles away; Themba's wayward sister enjoyed not a pauper's funeral, but a full-scale Shongwe send-off, with a hundred people staying overnight and being fed.

When Dokta's wife returned home to her mother, and his children moved into Themba's house, Lynn said, 'It's not fair. I don't see why the whole responsibility falls on Themba's shoulders.' But Themba knew what his obligations were. Like all forty-year-old Swazi men, Themba looked forward to retirement. When his sons and the girls were earning, this would become practicable. Swazi children, especially sons as heirs, are in lifelong debt to their parents. The way they discharge this debt is a matter of honour, not contract, but the investment in their education is almost calculable. Parents are likely to be the direct beneficiaries of the enhanced wages that their children's higher education is expected to achieve.

ஐ ௦

It is not surprising that Robert's impression was of poor people, lacking modern conveniences, leading a hand-to-mouth existence. Conspicuous consumption is the last thing on traditional Swazi minds. On the contrary, inconspicuous consumption is the aim. Only thus are the destructive forces of jealousy and envy kept at bay. Only the educated urban young, corrupted by commercial advertising, wear their clothing labels conspicuously on their shirt sleeves.

Robert's first instinct was to reach into his pocket. He wanted to open a bank account for the Shongwes, to help them buy a tractor, a car, to get electricity, a telephone, a government grant. They were undeveloped, but the potential was there, in the fertile land and the boundless free water. 'They're living on a gold mine,' said Lynn. 'I saw it from my first week here,' commented Robert. The Nestors' ambitions for the Shongwes were as old as colonialism. Robert thought he knew what they needed: capital.

He quickly hit upon a well-worn idea: proper freehold title to the share of Nation Land they had been allocated, in order to be able to use it as collateral to borrow money. But against ongoing pressure from development agencies, the wise old men of Swaziland, who have the final say, are holding firm against this proposal to do away with common land. Title to land would, of course, enable people to borrow from banks, to change their system of production from subsistence to commerce. It would just as surely see the ownership of land move steadily into the hands of the successful few and the creditors, as the land pledged against debt by the less successful was steadily repossessed.

Title to land is the route to the creation of a landless class. There is, as yet, no rootless urban working class in Swaziland. Every urban man has his eye on some rural land where he either has, or hopes to have, his homestead – whether by inheritance or fealty, *kukhonta*. And since to get this he must marry, women too get to share the security and bounty of the land. Permanently unmarried women are the only losers, and even they can eventually get access through their sons, if not through their fathers. The system discriminates as much by marital status as it does by sex. Single men are almost as powerless in the matter of access to land as single women. Childless unmarried women are seriously disadvantaged, but they are very few in number.

The wise old men of Swaziland have also been resisting the second part of Robert's vision for at least half a century – the commercial farming of king's land. They insist that this land is for the people's own use, as a source of homestead food, not profit. Mankind being imperfect, the system sometimes fails and rich men emerge, but the structures to redress inequalities are always in place. Land holdings are scrutinized every time a homestead head dies.

The Nestors wanted to change what they-called 'the cattle thing'. In typical Western fashion, they were unable to see the Shongwes' cattle as anything other than meat. Lynn called them 'forty head of prime beef' and could not understand why the Shongwes did not sell or eat them. It was like having a safe and losing the key. Although they knew that cattle were needed for marriage, for acquiring rights to children and land, and for paying healers, it was difficult to believe that money would not serve equally well. The Shongwes, however, viewed their cattle in terms of obligations honoured and yet to be honoured, exchanges made and yet to be made, which would create and sustain what the Nestors increasingly recognized, and admired, as a complex community.

Lynn's goal for the Shongwes was that they should be able to get off the homestead quickly: to go shopping, to the clinic, to drive the children to school, especially on rainy days. She thought they could buy an off-road vehicle for about ten cattle. But in southern Africa vehicles are relatively more expensive than they are in Britain, which is why vehicle theft is such big business. Ten cattle, at £120 each, would not buy a quarter of a serviceable second-hand four-wheel-drive vehicle. The cost of simply running such a vehicle would eat into the Shongwes' precious cash resources. Simultaneously, their potential income would fall as the number of calves born to their smaller herd fell. They would have less milk, less fertilizer. They might have trouble finding a team of six mature oxen to pull the sledge and plough. They might become poor.

Robert's proposal was more creative, but its economics were shaky. He thought the Shongwes should sell some cattle to buy a tractor, which would result in an agricultural surplus that they could sell in order to get electricity, a car and a television. He assumed (against the evidence on yields per acre) that traditional farming using ox ploughs is less productive than tractor ploughing. With no agricultural experience, he understandably did not take into account the surplus of homestead labour, how short the ploughing season is and how many months a tractor would stand idle; or the community pressures against commercial production on Nation Land. But above all, he took no account of tractor prices. The Shongwes would be lucky to find a second-hand tractor for the price of their entire herd. New tractors start at well over the value of a hundred cows.

The Shongwes share the Nestors' vision of an electrified homestead at Ekudzeni. They are well on their way to obtaining it through a community electrification scheme. The acting chief tried to explain to Robert, on his introductory visit at the end of January, that the Shongwes, along with several other homesteads in Ekudzeni, were paying monthly into a community fund for the chiefdom's electrification scheme, and had been doing so for years. Fewer than 20 per cent of Swazi households have electricity, and these are concentrated in the towns, but the government is committed in principle to putting electricity within everybody's reach. Ugly pylons now march across the countryside.

Make Shongwe thinks it will look nice to have the homestead lit up at night, to be able to look across the yard and see *gogo* laKhanyile's house and kitchen glowing in the dark. She also wants to keep light and warm the shed in which she plans to breed broilers. *Babe* Shongwe dreams of evenings in front of the television after a hard day's work. Lynn thought television represented the way forward for the whole country, since once people had television, she said, they would be exposed to a completely different way of life, which would make them want to change. *Make* Shongwe's broilers may be the agents of the very civilization that she dreads.

৪০ ৫ঃ

After eight weeks in Africa, Robert was ready to leave. 'I want my reality back. I've done the no electricity, tap at the end of the garden. We're in some frigging little hut, stuck out in a homestead. It's our ninth week. I want a shower and a fridge. I want to get back to normal. It's time for me to check out.'

Robert commented, 'This environment is a whole world away from where we actually live. The people are similar. The only difference is that we have more disposable income than the Shongwes do.' However, as in most British families, the Nestors' income (far from being disposable) is spent before it reaches their bank account and barely covers the cost of their Western lifestyle, with two cars and a mortgage. Robert says, 'I struggle to pay the mortgage. I never have any money. The direct debits at the bank are like a black hole. I only see money when I work extra at weekends.'

Lynn pondered their experience and was also ready to go back to London. She said she had no need of the shower, the electricity or the fridge, but she did need to be within ten minutes of the centre of town – any town. Lynn had discovered that nurses in Swaziland actually have relatively more disposable income than she has. Quizzing them about their salaries and expenses, she exclaimed in surprise, 'You're better off than I am, and I don't have a maid!' She had put her finger on an important part of the explanation: they had no mortgages and paid no rent. 'People here don't have to worry about a roof over their heads.'

She could see herself living on a homestead, running a rural clinic, but it would have to be one closer to town than the Shongwes'; and she would have to have a car, and an income that allowed her to put the children in private schools. Daniel would not want to come back, she said, except perhaps in his gap year. 'There'd be a tremendous protest if I said we were coming back to Ekudzeni. Robert could live an ex-pat life over here, right in the middle of Manzini, with a swimming pool.'

Robert had certainly noticed with a certain envy the lifestyle of the expatriates who 'come here wedged up with a lot of money. They can live good – and they do live good.' But he identified with the Swazis, not the expatriates. 'I struggled to get a job like they do. I haven't just strolled in. I struggle in England too.'

Back in London Robert said, 'I thought I was a tourist, but it was nothing like being a tourist on the homestead. Now I've come back, I can really see what I'm going to miss. At the time you take it for granted. When I'm driving around London, and it's chaotic and I'm stuck in traffic, I'll think of climbing a mountain, with Themba shouting a mile and a half off to a man with a gun; or going to the top of the homestead and just shouting to Dokta, and seeing him coming up from his house and saying, "Yes, I'm here." I'll think of the tree at the cattle dip, and I'll think, "I wish I was there now."'

INDEX